Colour Photography

COLLINS NUTSHELL BOOKS

Colour Photography

CHRISTOPHER TRENT

Illustrated in Colour

COLLINS
LONDON AND GLASGOW

First published 1962
Latest reprint 1969

Contents

FOREWORD

Every year more photographs are being taken in colour. Colour flatters the beginner, and there is no reason why the amateur should not take excellent colour pictures providing that he has mastered the first principles of his hobby.

This book has been written to give an easy introduction to these first principles in non-technical language. Only fuller experience can fill the inevitable gaps in the information provided. However, it is hoped with some confidence that amateurs with no previous experience of working in colour can produce pleasing pictures with the guidance this book offers.

Special emphasis has been laid on the choice of a camera and of the film to be used with it, because these two factors determine the results which the photographer can hope to obtain. The principles of composition in relation to colour—quite different from those applicable to monochrome photography—are also covered. The needs of beginners, and those who have had little experience with colour, have been kept in mind throughout.

My thanks are due to many people who have helped me to compile this book but especially to Richard Sheekey, who from his vast knowledge of photography and photographic equipment has made a number of corrections and valuable suggestions both at the manuscript and proof stages.

CHAPTER 1

The Choice of Camera

The choice of a camera is the most important factor in the making of good photographs, whether in monochrome or in colour. A number of special problems face the amateur in colour photography when making this choice because although it is true that any and every camera is capable of taking colour photographs in suitable conditions, very many of the cameras most suitable for black and white photography are less suitable for colour, due to the size of the pictures produced by them.

In recent years, the miniature camera using 35 mm. film and giving a negative of 36 mm. × 24 mm. has become dominant in the field of colour photography, for the simple reason that it is far less expensive to use than any other type. These 35 mm. cameras are best adapted to producing colour transparencies, which can either be viewed in a specially designed viewer or projected on to a screen. Because of its relatively low cost this type of colour photography has swept the world.

The price of colour films, including processing, varies, but with the 20 or 36 exposure cassette the cost of each transparency ready for viewing or projection is not in excess of a shilling, while one or two films recently introduced make colour photography even cheaper. When this cost is compared with that of black and white films, together with their processing and enlargement, it is obvious that the cost of colour photography, using optical instruments of the 35 mm. type, is not more expensive than that of photography in monochrome. All that is needed for colour photography, then, is a 35 mm. camera, and either a viewer, or a projector and screen.

Another factor which has made the 35 mm. size by far the most popular is that the equipment which goes with it has become standard and is mass-produced. A number of good projectors are available at relatively low cost. A number of viewers can be purchased for a price as low as a few shillings, while the great demand for the miniature camera has resulted in the production of many models by well known and reliable firms at much less cost than a few years ago. It is probably no exaggeration to say that more than 90 per cent of all colour photographs are taken with 35 mm. cameras.

35 mm. transparencies are mounted in card or glass holders which are $2'' \times 2''$, and it is for this size of mount that the standard projector or viewer is made. The square format allows upright or horizontal pictures to be accommodated.

Before colour photography became as popular as it is to-day the $2\frac{1}{4}'' \times 2\frac{1}{4}''$ negative, 12 on 120 or 620, was widely used and this size seemed likely to surpass in popularity both the miniature negative and the older $3\frac{1}{4}'' \times 2\frac{1}{4}''$ negative, 8 on 120 or 620. So many people possessed cameras tied to this size of negative, that the manufacturers were convinced of the necessity of catering for their needs. The result is that several viewers are available for $2\frac{1}{4}'' \times 2\frac{1}{4}''$ transparencies. Transparencies produced by the $2\frac{1}{4}'' \times 2\frac{1}{4}''$ cameras are normally mounted in holders measuring $2\frac{3}{4}'' \times 2\frac{3}{4}''$. The transparency size is often called 6 cm. $\times$ 6 cm., while the mounts are 7 cm. $\times$ 7 cm. Several modern types of camera, however, are sold with a mask which reduces slightly the size of the transparency so that it can be mounted to fit into the conventional type of 35 mm. projector. The slides so produced are called " super slides," and are exactly the same size as those produced by cameras taking 12 exposures on 127 size film. The drawback of these " super slides," of course, is that they are square, which is not really the most suitable format, though it is often most effective for photographs of people. Several projectors also have been introduced to accommodate the larger slides of the $2\frac{1}{4}'' \times 2\frac{1}{4}''$ format in their standard mounts.

A relatively small number of photographers aim at the production of negatives from which only paper prints can be made. Their needs are entirely different from those of photographers who are content with transparencies which can be viewed through a viewer or projected on to a screen. In their case the larger the size of the negative, the better. The old style $3\frac{1}{4}'' \times 2\frac{1}{4}''$ negative, i.e. 8 on 120 or 620, is by far the best medium. We shall have a great deal more to say about the difference between films from which transparencies can be made and those from which paper prints are made in the following chapter, but it is worth noting that paper prints, coloured photographs on paper, can be made easily from any transparency, and the cost of doing this is little more than that of making paper prints from negatives. The only advice which can be given to the beginner who is concerned with the cost of colour photography, is to concentrate on transparencies, which can be used as slides to be viewed or projected but from which prints can be made if desired.

First, we must consider the relative merits of some of the vast number of miniature 35 mm. cameras which are on sale. It is not surprising that the choice appears very difficult to a beginner, seeing that there are over two hundred models available, and that these range in price from less than £7 to more than £250. What precisely is one looking for? What are the advantages of an expensive camera over a cheaper one?

A camera in its basic form is an extremely simple piece of

11

mechanism. It consists of a box into which no light can penetrate unless a button is pushed or a lever pulled. The front is occupied by an optical lens, the back by a carrier over which film, sensitive to light, is transported. Between the lens and the film there is a metal shutter which prevents light reaching the film except when the shutter is raised or drawn aside.

In all except the most simple cameras, there is also a diaphragm which regulates the amount of light which reaches the film when the shutter is open by varying the proportion of the lens which is exposed to the light. The larger the aperture of the lens, the more light will penetrate to the film; the smaller the aperture of the lens, the less light will reach the film.

Similarly the longer the barrier between the lens and the film is removed, the greater will be the amount of light transmitted to it. All the more expensive cameras allow the user to vary the amount of light transmitted by either means. The whole lens may be exposed to the light for a brief period, or a small part for a longer period. The result in terms of light transmitted may be the same but there are great advantages in transmitting light for a longer period through a smaller aperture because that results in a greater depth of field, that is to say, objects in the foreground and background of a picture can be in focus, whereas if the whole lens is used only objects precisely in focus will appear sharp in the finished picture.

Competition among the manufacturers of cameras in Britain, Germany, and other countries, is intense. It can be assumed, therefore, that any camera on the market is good value for money. The real difference between a cheap camera and a more expensive one is that the more expensive one has greater versatility. It has a lens capable of introducing varying amounts of light to the film and a shutter which will give exposures of more varying duration.

So the more expensive camera will make it possible to take satisfactory photographs in a greater variety of light conditions than a cheaper one. It will also make it possible to obtain clear images of a wider variety of subjects.

In most cases, the expensive camera will also have a better lens, which gives clearer definition and will permit a greater degree of enlargement without loss of detail. The short exposures which are possible with the more elaborate cameras fitted with the most modern types of shutter, also make it possible to take good photographs of rapidly moving subjects such as horses galloping, or even racing cars on the track—outside the scope of a simple camera.

Apart from these factors there is no essential difference between the modest box camera and the most elaborate and costly instruments available. A number of the more expensive cameras have built-in accessories, particularly range-finders and photo-electric exposure meters. A range-finder, which enables one to focus the camera on the main subject of interest in a picture, is very nearly essential for any photograph except subjects for which the simplest box cameras are designed, such as groups of people on the beach (which is, after all, the most popular subject for holiday snapshots). An exposure meter, an instrument which measures the intensity of the light falling upon the subject, is also very useful, but it must always be borne in mind that relatively cheap range finders and exposure meters can be purchased separately and although their separate use takes a little longer than it would if they were built into the camera, the pictures which result may be just as good.

It all depends, therefore, on how much one can afford to pay for a camera. The cheapest box camera is capable of producing acceptable transparencies or colour prints in bright sunshine on the beach, or in other places which are without shadows, but nothing more. The more expensive instruments are capable of producing good colour photographs, whether transparencies or prints, in almost any light in summer or winter.

Another point which ought to be stressed when the purchase of a camera is contemplated is that there is no such thing as a professional camera except, perhaps, the highly specialised plate cameras which can only be used with a rigid tripod. For all practical purposes any hand-held camera, whether it is a box camera at £3 or a Hasselblad at nearly £300, is as suitable for the amateur as it is for the professional. Many professional photographers use cameras such as the Rolleiflex, which are primarily designed for amateurs, and there is no real distinction between the two types.

Only a few years ago it was said that the best cameras on sale in Great Britain and the United States, and indeed in all countries of the world, were of German manufacture. Recently, with the enormous increase in the use of colour, British manufacturers have marketed a wide range of cameras specially adapted to take colour photographs in the 35 mm. range and these, price for price, are at least equal in value to the best German models. In the more expensive price range a number of excellent Japanese and Russian cameras have also been introduced.

One of the most interesting ranges of cameras manufactured in Britain is that marketed by the Kodak Company. The box Brownie of pre-war days has grown up and for colour enthusiasts has been replaced by the Brownie 44A and 44B. Both cameras represent exceptional value for money and both are perfectly suitable for taking colour pictures, providing the light is good. Both are adequate for recording memorable scenes on seaside or country holidays providing it is not desired to take difficult landscapes, or subjects in shadow or in cloudy weather conditions.

The 44A is marketed at less than £3. It takes twelve pictures on 127 film, each picture $1\frac{9}{16}'' \times 1\frac{9}{16}''$, i.e. making it possible to project the transparencies on a standard 35 mm. projector. For a camera of its price it has several unexpected refinements, for instance a built-in flash contact for use as an accessory flash holder, so that snapshots can be taken indoors as well. It has a large eye-level view-finder—easier to use than many fitted on expensive cameras. The lens is a simple one with two aperture settings but a drawback inherent in all inexpensive cameras is that the focus is fixed. This means that although excellent results can be obtained from the kind of subject which holiday snapshotters most often take—little Henry building a sand castle, mother and father asleep in deck chairs on the beach, a group of people outside a guest house—exact definition cannot be expected in landscapes or distant objects, since the area of sharpest definition is between 12 and 20 feet. Similarly, close-ups are not really a practical proposition.

Some of these drawbacks are overcome in the Brownie 44B, which costs less than £5. This camera also takes twelve square pictures on 127 film. The lens is an $f/8$ with additional stops at $f/11$ and $f/16$, making it possible to give the right exposure for almost any subject in bright lighting conditions.

Many beginners are puzzled by the custom of referring to lenses by their f number. f is an abbreviation for " factor " while the number attached represents the proportion between the focal length of the lens and its diameter. In other words, the f number used determines the amount of light which reaches the lens. Lenses with a low f number are faster than those with a high f number. They allow more light to reach the lens and, therefore, require a shorter exposure.

Many years ago agreement was reached between the

manufacturers of cameras on an international basis to standardise the values. The present position, with very few exceptions, is that each f number engraved on the front of the camera represents a speed twice as fast as the next larger number. On all except the more expensive cameras the numbers engraved are 5·6, 8, 11, 16 and 22 or some of these. If you choose an aperture of $f/11$ and an exposure of 1/100th of a second with a fast film in bright sunshine you can use an aperture of $f/16$ with an exposure of 1/50th of a second using the same film in the same lighting conditions. Some of the most expensive cameras have extremely fast lenses, for instance $f/1·5$. There are quite a number of miniature cameras of moderate cost which have an $f/2·8$ lens.

Versatility is given to the Brownie 44B by the focusing scale, which is marked from infinity to 3 feet, and there are settings for views, groups, and close-ups. These three settings are in line with the recent tendency to make it easier for the beginner to achieve the right focus without a range-finder or without measuring the distance exactly. This camera also has a two-speed shutter, 1/30th and 1/60th of a second, and in addition a brief time setting.

All these refinements give the 44B a much greater versatility than the 44A but it must be stressed that 1/30th of a second is a longer time than many people can hold a camera still so as to ensure pin sharp reproduction. Even 1/60th is not easy and many professionals never use a speed slower than 1/100th of a second, while any attempt to hold a camera still for a brief time exposure is doomed to failure. It follows that it is a very great help to good photography with inexpensive cameras if some support can be found for the camera to make it easier to hold it completely still, such as a gate or a wall. The alternative is to grip the camera firmly, press it against the face if it

This charming study of children at a window was an *Encyclopædia Britannica* Award winner. It captures perfectly the mood of the children, who are entirely unself-conscious. *Kodak Ektachrome film. Photo by John Drysdale.*

The reds and greens and blues combine to make a fine colour rendering of the lovely landscape in Glendalough in County Wicklow,
Ireland. *Kodak Ektachrome film. Photo by J. Allen Cash.*

has an eye-level viewer, and deliberately hold the breath while the exposure is being made. People differ in their ability to remain absolutely motionless for a brief period and only experience can show how long this period is for each individual.

That is one of the chief drawbacks of this kind of camera, apart from the fact that inevitably the definition of which the lens is capable is not so precise as that of lenses five or even ten times as expensive. When one remembers that the cost of a really high quality lens itself may be £50, the extraordinary value offered by cameras of this kind is immediately apparent.

There are two even cheaper cameras which can produce fair results. One Kodak model, for instance, costs little more than £1. The makers claim for this model that there are absolutely no adjustments to be made. That is only too true. It is a fixed focus single-speed camera with the simplest of lenses. Unfortunately it takes 8 pictures on 127 film and, therefore, is not really suitable for the making of transparencies, though good results can be obtained with film such as Kodacolor, producing negatives from which colour paper prints are made. In spite of this it cannot be recommended with confidence to amateurs whose chief interest is likely to be in taking colour pictures because of the relatively greater expense of producing colour prints. Another Brownie Camera, which costs little more than £2, takes 12 pictures on the 120/620 size of film. These pictures can be enjoyed with the help of one of the several viewers manufactured to accommodate the $2\frac{1}{4}'' \times 2\frac{1}{4}''$ size, or by projection with one of the recently introduced projectors which accept transparencies of this size. The advantage of this model is that it has an $f/11$ lens which can be stopped down to $f/16$. It also has flash contacts for indoor pictures with an accessory flash holder, and the built-in close-up lens enables pictures of

17

exceptional quality to be taken of objects only 4 feet away from the photographer.

The Kodak range also includes cameras specially designed for working in colour—the Colorsnap range. The cheaper model is equipped with an $f/3\cdot9$ lens. A great advantage for beginners is that an exposure guide for daylight and flash pictures is built into the back of the camera. The weather dial exposure chart is marked for bright sun, hazy sun, cloudy bright, and cloudy dull. All that is necessary is to turn the pointer to the appropriate weather marking, read off the number shown, and set the camera to that number. The focus is adjustable for views, groups, and close-ups

Apart from the markings for close-ups, groups and views, the lens can be focused from 3 feet to infinity. The twelve transparencies produced from the 828 size film can be mounted in the standard $2'' \times 2''$ mounts and are, therefore, suitable for projection in the same way as " super slides." The exact size of the transparencies produced from 828 size film is $1\frac{9}{13}'' \times 1\frac{1}{8}''$— 40 mm. $\times$ 28 mm.— very little larger than the 36 mm. $\times$ 24 mm. of the standard 35 mm. frame. Altogether this is a remarkable camera for less than £10.

The more expensive model is even more versatile, and will provide, at certainly no more cost than any other camera, an introduction to the full possibilities of 35 mm. photography, in colour or black and white. The exposure guide on the camera back makes for fairly accurate exposure, the focusing dial is simple, the eye-level viewfinder adequate. It is fitted with a $f/3\cdot9$ lens, a fast enough lens to take almost any subject which the holiday photographer will want to take, a double exposure prevention device, as well as flash contacts and all the other features of Kodak cameras in general. It takes 20 or 36 transparencies from the standard 35 mm. cassettes and repre-

sents a genuine effort to produce a precision built miniature camera at a reasonable price.

The Kodak Company also distributes the Retinettes, two
more expensive cameras representing equally good value—
one at under £20, the other at less than £30. Both are
precision-built 35 mm. cameras, suited to the production
of colour transparencies for viewing or projection. Both
are fitted with an $f/2\cdot8$ Reomar lens. The cheaper model
is fitted with a Pronto shutter with speeds of 1/30th,
1/60th, 1/125th, and 1/250th of a second, the more expensive one with a more advanced Pronto shutter giving
exposures up to 1/500th. The eye-level view-finder is good
and easy to use, the movement of a single lever advances
the film, counts the exposures, and sets the shutter in both
cameras. Both are also fitted with the necessary attachments for taking flash pictures. Apart from the refinements
of the shutter, the chief difference between the two is that
the more expensive one has a built-in exposure meter
which gives an immediate answer to the question " what
exposure shall I give? " All that is necessary is to point
the camera at the subject to be photographed and centre
the exposure indicator needle in the view-finder. This
automatically adjusts the lens to give the correct exposure.
So this camera offers a marked degree of automation for
less than £30—a quite remarkable achievement.

The Ilford range of cameras for colour photography is
equally impressive. The Ilford equivalent of the Brownies
are the Sportis. The Sporti 4 uses 127 size film on which
12 pictures $1\frac{8}{16}'' \times 1\frac{9}{16}''$ are taken, suitable for mounting in
standard mounts and being projected. It costs less than
£3. It has a fixed focus lens which gives pictures which are
sharp from 6 feet to about 40 feet, but the shutter is a
single-speed one. Allowance, however, is made for sunny
and cloudy weather, the control varying the aperture
of the lens. There is an eye-level view-finder and a par-

ticularly easy press-button release. This is obviously a camera which should be considered carefully by any beginner and is equally adaptable to black and white or colour.

Two other Sporti models are the original Sporti and the Super Sporti. Both take 120 size film, producing 12 pictures from each film $2\frac{1}{4}'' \times 2\frac{1}{4}''$. These are unsuitable for projection on many standard projectors but can be viewed in the several viewers available for this size. The Sporti is as easy to use as any camera on the market. Like the Sporti 4 it incorporates a lever which can be set to sunny or cloudy, while the lens can be set to close-up, group, or view, to ensure a reasonable focus. The eye-level view-finder is similar to that on the Sporti 4 and the push-button release is reliable and smooth in action, reducing camera shake to a minimum.

The Super Sporti is the Sporti's big brother. It looks very similar, uses the same film, has the same view-finder and push-button shutter release, but incorporates a few refinements to give it greater versatility. Instead of two exposure settings, it has three, marked sunny, light cloud, and dull. It also has a double exposure prevention device, always an extremely valuable adjunct to a camera, especially if one is likely to take a number of photographs in quick succession. The price of the Sporti is slightly under £4, of the Super Sporti under £6 and both are excellent value.

The Ilford range, however, includes two cameras specially suitable for rather more advanced colour photography—the Sportsman and the Sportsmaster. Both are miniatures, taking 35 mm. cassettes, and incorporate a number of special features usually associated with much more expensive instruments. The price of the Sportsman is approximately £15, and of the Sportsmaster less than £30. There is also a more expensive version of the Sportsman which although still well under £20 includes a coupled range-finder.

The Standard Sportsman, generally known from the name of its shutter as the Vario, has an $f/2\cdot8$ lens and a three-speed shutter, giving an exposure as short as 1/200th of a second. The Range-Finder model has the same $f/2\cdot8$ lens but a four-speed shutter speeded to 1/250th of a second, making it easier to take swiftly moving objects, with a coupled range-finder and a delayed action mechanism. The Pronto shutter with speeds of 1/30th, 1/60th, 1/125th and 1/250th of a second gives a wide latitude in setting the exposure and the delayed action mechanism gives the photographer time to include himself in any group or scene which he is photographing.

Nothing need be said of the coupled range-finder except that it is extremely useful, especially for subjects near to the camera. The lens incorporated in all the Sportsman range is said to be particularly suitable for taking colour transparencies.

The Sportsmaster is a precision-built camera for enthusiastic amateurs and is one of the cheapest " automatic " cameras on the market. It is certainly true that automation may not be to the liking of some professionals, but it is a great advantage to beginners because one can be certain that the combination of exposure and diaphragm setting will be reasonably accurate. An automatic camera of this kind is as simple to use as a box camera, but vastly more versatile and capable of being used in a greatly increased range of lighting and other conditions and with far greater assurance that the picture will be correctly exposed.

The Sportsmaster incorporates a photo-electric exposure meter. It has the same $2\cdot8$ lens as the Sportsman and the same kind of view-finder. The manufacturers claim that by setting the Sportsmaster dial to the signs which represent respectively landscapes, groups, full-length portraits, and close-up portraits, the camera will do everything else that is required. The focusing positions are infinity for landscapes, 13 feet for groups, 8 feet for full-length portraits, and 5 feet for close-ups—which have been proved by experience to be most suitable for these four types of pictures. Moreover, as the photographer views his subject in the view-finder an optical light-strength signal tells him if there is enough light for a successful picture and so prevents wasting film. The shutter speed is determined when the film speed is pre-set on the appropriate scale, while the exposure meter decides on the aperture and transmits the information to the lens diaphragm, so that when the release button is pressed the correct aperture has been set automatically. Three new cameras in the Sportsman/Sportsmaster range have been introduced recently. Each of these three new models has the automatic exposure control pioneered by the original Sportsmaster. They range in price from less than £30 to about £45. The introduction of these new models brought the number of cameras in the Ilford range to eleven.

Among imported cameras the Paxette range competes with the Kodak and Ilford ranges. One model retailing at between £25 and £30 includes most advantages of the Sportsmaster and a fully reliable lens. It is described as a self-setting electric eye camera. It is a 35 mm. camera taking the normal 20 or 36 exposure cassettes. All the photographer has to do is to compose his subject in the view-finder and leave the light measured by the built-in electric exposure meter to determine the diaphragm/exposure setting. As in the Sportsmaster, there is a device which tells the user if the light is not sufficient for a properly exposed picture.

Another smaller camera, at a similar price, takes 12 pictures of $1\frac{9}{16}'' \times 1\frac{9}{16}''$ on 127 roll film. More elaborate forms of the same camera are also available at prices between £40 and £50.

The Super Paxette is a more advanced type of camera which incorporates the same features as the others in the range and also has the advantage of interchangeable lenses. It is claimed to be one of the cheapest 35 mm. cameras allowing the use of interchangeable lenses. Although it cannot be regarded as an inexpensive camera, the advantage of being able to use interchangeable lenses is a very great one for all amateurs who are keenly interested in making colour transparencies of the highest possible quality and interest. A wide-angle lens makes it possible to photograph a much greater range of subjects than is practicable with the normal lens. All photographers know of the advantage of the wide-angle lens in rendering landscapes but such a lens can be equally useful in photographing buildings, while professionals nearly always use wide-angle lenses for large groups, such as weddings and dinner parties. There is no reason why the amateur should not adopt the same technique as the professional in cases like these, or why the results achieved by the amateur should be inferior.

There is, indeed, no real distinction between an amateur and a professional photographer except that the latter more often possesses the finest kind of optical equipment and devotes his life to studying his subject, while the amateur is usually limited both in time and expense. However, the Super Paxette and some other cameras in a similar price range give the amateur the opportunity of experimenting with high-class equipment, including excellent lenses and shutters, two prime requirements for good photography, at a price which is relatively small.

The Super Paxette can be purchased with a variety of lenses. The cheapest lens is the Katagon 2·8. The price of the camera with this lens is at present only slightly in excess of £30, a Cassarit 2·8 lens is about £3 more, while the Super Paxette fitted with a Zeiss Xenar 2·8 lens is between £40 and £45, with a Zeiss Tessar 2·8 lens almost £50. The difference in price represents only the difference in the cost of the lenses and is a good guide to the quality.

One Super Paxette has a built-in photo-electric exposure meter as well as a coupled range-finder. The price of this model is approximately £13 more. If one wants a full range of lenses the capital expenditure is quite considerable. The cost of the wide-angle lens supplied to fit these cameras is in the region of £15, while telephoto lenses range between £10 and £40. It must be stressed that the advantages of a telephoto lens are immense.

If it is desired to take a photograph of Big Ben (St. Stephen's Tower) from the south bank of the Thames, very little detail can be obtained with the normal lens, yet with a telephoto lens the detail is extraordinary and the colour values far nearer to reality. The Super Paxette fitted with a standard Tessar lens and supplementary wide-angle and telephoto lenses can cost less than £100. A Prontor SVS nine-speed shutter is fitted as standard to this camera so that the special equipment for the amateur is as complete as possible and the colour pictures that can be taken in any reasonable light or situation cover as wide a range as he will be likely to require.

A more expensive and elaborate 35 mm. camera in the same range, the Super Paxette 3, combines automatic exposure with the same interchangeable system as the other Super Paxettes. It can be operated without having to estimate the lens aperture or exposure. Only focusing is left to the operator. There is no doubt that this degree of automation enables the most inexperienced amateur to obtain excellent results. It is no exaggeration to say hat such automatic cameras are as easy to operate as box cameras but give vastly superior results in widely differing conditions of light and situation. Moreover, on this model the coupled range-finder gives easily distinguishable images for the normal, wide-angle and telephoto lenses, while the Prontor SLK shutter allows speeds up to 1/300th of a second, fast enough to photograph without blur most moving objects.

Inevitably the cost is high. Fitted with an $f/1.9$ Ennalyt lens, the Super Paxette 3 costs between £75 and £80, while the accessory telephoto lens costs between £35 and £40, and the wide-angle lens is between £30 and £35. An economy can be made by buying a model fitted with an $f/2.8$ Ultralyt lens, the saving being rather more than £20. But it may be said that it is scarcely worth spoiling the ship for a ha'p'orth of tar, even though the halfpenny is more than £20. The difference between an $f/1.9$ lens and an $f/2.8$ lens is very great in bad light, especially indoors, when it is not possible to use a flash gun or photofloods.

Many references are made in this chapter to reflex cameras. The term reflex is a rather misleading one. What it means is that cameras of this type, instead of having the usual view-finder, with or without a range-finder, present a picture in colour on a ground glass screen to enable the photographer to compose his picture and to focus it precisely. There is no doubt that a reflex camera makes it easier for the beginner and the more experienced amateur to compose a satisfactory picture, especially in colour, seeing that the image in the screen is in natural colour and he can tell without any possibility of doubt exactly what is going to be reproduced in his transparency or colour negative.

The difference between a single-lens and a twin-lens reflex camera is principally one of method. A single-lens reflex uses the same lens for viewing as for photographing, a twin-lens reflex has two separate lenses, one used only for viewing the picture in the screen, the other for making the exposure. Each type has its advocates, the single-lens variety being preferred by some because most single-lens reflex cameras are adapted to accept interchangeable lenses—telephoto, wide-angle, close-up—whereas twin-lens models are not normally so adapted. In any case the main advantage of both types of camera is that they allow the photographer to see a " proof " of his picture before he actually takes it.

An interesting addition to the range of 35 mm. cameras has been made by the Agfa Company with the Flexilette, which brings 35 mm. colour photography into the world of the twin-lens reflex at relatively small expense. Agfa have produced many fine cameras but few more versatile than this one. It is fitted with identical $f/2\cdot8$ Agfacolor Apotar lenses for viewing and taking, especially designed for colour work but equally suitable for photography in black and white. It has a very competent range-finder, a Prontor shutter with speeds from one second to 1/500th, the usual interlocking mechanism to prevent double or blank exposure, and many other refinements, but its chief merit for the amateur is its reflex view finder, which gives a clear image of the subject to be taken in its natural colours.

It is quite impossible within the scope of a small book to list all the cameras available to the amateur, still less to give any precise indication of their particular qualities and of the results which they can be expected to achieve, but there are four types of advanced cameras which demand mention, if only because they are used by so many amateurs to good effect. These are the Vito and Zeiss ranges, the Leica, and the Rolleiflex.

The Vito range includes cameras varying in price from less than £20 to more than £50. One which offers exceptionally good value is a handsome 35 mm. camera with an unusually efficient view-finder, an $f/2\cdot8$ lens, and a shutter which gives exposures ranging from 1/25th to 1/250th of a second. At less than £20 this represents remarkable value. The Vito CD is similar in appearance and in much of its equipment but is fitted with a photo-electric exposure meter which has proved reliable in practice and is semi-automatic in use. Like so many other cameras in its class it has what are called zone focusing marks for portraits, groups and views. A more advanced model has all the same features but a more versatile shutter which gives exposures from 1/15th to 1/500th of a second, while another model has a coupled range-finder, and built-in photo-electric exposure meter coupled to the shutter setting ring.

The Vitomatic IA and IIA are in the same tradition as the Vitos but rather more versatile and more expensive. The only important difference between them is that the IIA has a coupled range-finder, whereas the IA has not. Both have built-in exposure meters, the indicators of which are visible in the view-finder, so that the aperture can be set while the camera is at eye level. Both are fitted with a $f/2\cdot8$ lens and a shutter giving exposures of one second to 1/500th. The exposure meter is coupled to the aperture/shutter setting. There is a very useful depth of field indicator and the same zone focusing system as on the simpler models. The price of the Vitomatic IA is approximately £45; of the IIA model approximately £55.

Not everyone would agree that the names Leica, Rolleiflex and Zeiss represent the finest equipment available to the amateur photographer. But certainly no one would question the statement that these ranges of cameras, embracing as they do half a century of experience and research, give the amateur in colour photography almost everything that he could desire, and at a competitive price, even though that price may appear high. All three ranges of cameras have first-class bodies, excellent lenses and shutters, and all the accessories which make so much difference to successful photography.

To take the Zeiss range first, a number of fairly cheap cameras are marketed under the Zeiss trade-mark which are competitive with those that have been mentioned before. One of the most interesting of these is the Zeiss Colora 35 mm. fitted with a 3·5 lens and four-speed shutter giving exposures from 1/30th to 1/250th of a second, for less than £20. But there are two fairly recent 35 mm. cameras which, though expensive, incorporate every possible aid to good photography, the Super Contaflex and the Contarex. The Super Contaflex costs rather more than £100, the Contarex about £250, a very expensive camera, yet one which incorporates every possible aid for the amateur. The Super Contaflex is a single lens reflex camera with a built-in photo-electric exposure meter linked to the Synchro-Compur shutter, with meter indications visible in the view-finder and on the body of the camera. It is fitted with an f/2·8 Tessar lens and will accept wide-angle and telephoto auxiliary lenses.

The Contarex is also a single-lens reflex camera with a built-in exposure meter coupled to the aperture and speed settings, and will accept any of the Zeiss interchangeable lenses. It has a shutter speeded from one second to 1/1,000th of a second and is fitted in the standard model with an f/2 Planar lens which focuses down to 12 inches. It is not without reason that the manufacturers describe the Contarex as the most magnificent photographic instrument of its kind in the world. Its mechanical and optical precision is superb. The view-finder shows exactly what appears on the negative or the transparency. As the exposure meter is coupled both to the shutter and the speed setting, either shutter speed or aperture may be pre-selected. However, the coupling can be disconnected when required and allow the user to determine his own setting of speed and aperture, quite irrespective of the exposure meter, a great advantage in some landscape pictures in which it is almost impossible to obtain a true reading from an exposure meter.

The Rolleiflex is world famous. Formerly, Rolleiflex cameras and even their young brothers, the Rolleicords, were regarded as luxury cameras but in recent years a number of cheaper models have come on the market which incorporate many of the features which have established the Rolleiflex reputation.

Rolleiflex and Rolleicord cameras take twelve exposures on 120 film, It can be assumed that every camera which bears the name has a first-class lens and an excellent shutter. One of the cheapest at the moment is the Rolleiflex T, which is fitted with a 3·5 Tessar lens and is in many ways the ideal instrument for the amateur who is prepared to spend upwards of £75 on his camera and its essential accessories such as lens hoods, masking equipment, and filters. All Rolleiflex cameras have one thing in common, namely a ground-glass focusing screen in which the subject to be photographed can be viewed in natural colours, and by merely rotating a knob the best focusing position can be chosen. They are all simple in operation. The main difference between one model and another is the versatility of the lens and other equipment.

Quite recently a new model has been introduced, the Rolleimagic, which is as simple to use as a box camera and yet incorporates all the refinements necessary to make first-class transparencies. In appearance it is almost identical with the other models but all calculations of exposures are carried out automatically by the camera, which quite literally " thinks " for the user. All that is necessary is to aim the camera at the subject to be photographed, focus in the ground-glass screen, and press the shutter release. The automatic action of the exposure meter selects the shutter speed and the aperture, ideal for the user who is interested in pictorial quality but not in technicalities. Fitted with a 3·5 Xenar lens, it is only a little more expensive than the Rolleiflex T.

Leica cameras have achieved a remarkable reputation for reliability as well as for the excellence of their optical equipment. Many who have used a Leica would never exchange it for any other make. It is certainly true that all Leica 35 mm. cameras are ideal for colour photography when transparencies for viewing or projection are desired. It was recently pointed out by the owner of the 62nd Leica camera marketed in Great Britain that the camera was still giving excellent service, was said to be as good as when it was purchased 35 years ago, and was taking pictures as sharp as those produced by modern cameras costing five or six times as much as the Leica did then.

A relatively expensive camera can be an investment for a lifetime. The most recent range of Leicas include two cameras, the M2 and the M3, which are as suitable for the amateur photographer in colour as any 35 mm. camera on the market. Both have view-finders which are coupled to built-in range-finders for automatic focusing and a focal plane shutter with speeds from one second to 1/1,000th of a second coupled to a photo-electric exposure meter. Both are marketed with a variety of lenses. The M2, fitted with an $f/2\cdot8$ Elmar, is retailed at approximately £120, with an $f/2$ Summicron at just over £150, and with an $f/1\cdot4$ Summilux at approximately £180. The M3 with equivalent lenses is about £20 more expensive.

This chapter has described only a few of the superb optical instruments available to the enthusiast, who may wish to consider many other cameras with features similar to those described above. There is, for instance, the Agima, which for about £30 provides an $f/2\cdot8$ lens, a shutter with ten speeds, and a coupled range-finder, with an interchangeable telephoto lens for an additional £12. There is the Halina, which has an $f/3\cdot5$ lens, a four-speed shutter, and an all-metal body for less than £8. There is the Periflex Gold Star range, which for about £50 gives an $f/2\cdot8$ lens or for a few pounds more an $f/1\cdot9$ lens, with interchangeable wide-angle and telephoto lenses available.

There are the recently arrived Russian cameras, such as the Zenith C, with an $f/3\cdot5$ lens and a shutter with speeds from 1/30th to 1/500th of a second—a single-lens reflex camera—for about £30, and for twice that sum a camera known as the Kiev 4 with a built-in exposure meter, a coupled range-finder, an $f/2$ lens, and a shutter with speeds from half a second to 1/1,250th of a second.

A number of Japanese cameras are also being imported. The performance of some of these is exceptional, although the prices are not materially less than for comparable cameras manufactured in Germany or Great Britain. One deserves special mention, the 35 mm. Olympus Auto Eye, retailing at about £40, which can be used either as a fully automatic or a conventional manually set type. It is fitted with an $f/2\cdot8$ lens and a nine-speed shutter and has a fully coupled exposure meter for automatic aperture and shutter adjustment and a coupled range-finder combined with the view-finder. Clearly this represents exceptional value. Another model which has been highly praised is the Minolta A5, a 35 mm. camera with an $f/2\cdot8$ lens and a shutter allowing exposures from one second to 1/1,000th of a second. An unusual focusing device permits focusing from less than 3 feet to infinity—all at a price of approximately £35.

Among the hundreds of imported cameras none is better value than the most simple type of the Werra range. For rather less than £20 it is possible to buy a Werra camera which incorporates an $f/2\cdot8$ Tessar lens, one of the finest in the world, and an eight-speed shutter with a built-in lens hood. The shutter and the lens alone are worth more than the whole camera at current prices. Moreover a leather case is not necessary for the effective use of this camera which is supplied with a convenient neck strap. More expensive models with interchangeable lenses and coupled range-finders are available but none of these represents such remarkable value as the Model I, which is surely the cheapest camera incorporating a really first-class lens and a first-class shutter.

In any case, whatever camera the beginner or the more experienced amateur decides to buy, the lens and the shutter are its two most important components. Built-in exposure meters, coupled range-finders, and the like, are all useful but not essential to taking a good photograph; nothing can take the place of a good lens and shutter. Those are the two things to look for in any camera. Although it is true that a good photographer can take acceptable pictures with any camera, while a bad photographer cannot take good pictures with the finest camera in the world, a reliable shutter and a discriminating lens are absolutely essential if transparencies are to be produced in varying conditions and in varying light, from the brightest of sunny summer days to the dullest of dark days in the winter.

The combination of human and animal interest suggests many ideas for attractive photographs. Here the red of the girl's dress is the dominant colour factor and is effective in preventing the picture from being " stolen " by the horse. *Kodak Kodachrome film.*

An attractive Nigerian girl demonstrates one of her dances. Such colourful scenes of other lands remind us that it is always worth taking a camera when travelling abroad on business or pleasure. *Kodak Ektachrome film. Photo by David Johnson.*

CHAPTER 2

The Choice of Film

If the choice of a camera is the most important factor which will make for taking good pictures in colour, the choice of film is certainly the next most important. It cannot be said that one particular film is more suitable than another for any particular make of camera, although it is true that with simple cameras, especially box-type, the faster the film the larger the number of subjects there are which can be photographed without under-exposure. Apart from that, the choice of film is largely a matter of personal preference based on experience.

The best plan is to find the film giving the results which appeal most strongly to the individual photographer, and then stick to it. There is really very little difference between the various films available except that some render one colour more faithfully, others another. The slower films generally give less " graininess " than the fast ones while the faster films give rather more latitude, which means that a slightly under-exposed or over-exposed picture is more acceptable than if it were taken on slower film. Even this is not a firm rule, because some of the slower films allow a far greater latitude than is generally supposed.

Latitude is a relative word. Most professional photographers agree that in colour rendering there is very little latitude at all, whatever film is used, certainly not more than half a stop, while calculating the best exposure in any situation is extraordinarily difficult. The literature issued with almost all colour films is extremely helpful but no manufacturer would claim that the exposure time and/or aperture recommended is precisely right. The exposure/ aperture recommendation is the average which will produce fair results in the conditions described and for the kind of subject to be photographed. Even a photo-electric exposure meter cannot be relied upon in all circumstances, for various reasons, especially when photographing landscapes, when the amount of light from the sky reaching the exposure meter is often much greater than the light reflected by the landscape. We shall have more to say about the use of exposure meters later.

In choosing a film obviously the most important decision to make is whether to use a reversal or a negative film. As has been said already, negative films produce negatives from which positive colour prints on paper are made, while reversal films produce transparencies which can either be viewed in a viewer or projected on a screen. The paper prints from negative films can be enlarged in the same way as monochrome photographs but the cost is relatively high. If, for instance, one is using a 120/620 camera taking 8 pictures on a roll, the cost of developing and printing is more than a pound, while a 5″ × 7″ enlargement will cost upwards of 12/-. En-prints approximately $3\frac{1}{2}″ \times 5″$ cost between 2/- and 3/-. Although results are not always successful, it must be remembered that colour prints on paper can be made from transparencies and the cost of these is little more than that of enlargements from negative films. Prints of $3\frac{1}{2}″ \times 5″$ are made by Kodak and Ilford from transparencies for less than 3/- each, while enlargements of 5″ × 7″ cost between 7/6 and 10/6. (Not all film manufacturers, however, provide this service.) The most economical film, therefore, is 35 mm. reversal film.

Whether the film chosen is of the reversal or negative type, the principle underlying its use is the same. The film material is coated with three separate layers of light-sensitive emulsions, in contrast with monochrome films which are coated with only one layer. The first of these layers is sensitive to blue, the second to yellow, and the third to red. The two layers which record the yellow and red light are also sensitive to blue. In order to prevent blue light filtering through to them, they are separated from the uppermost layer, that is, the layer sensitive to blue, by a filter. A great deal of the effectiveness of colour films depends on how efficient this filter is. Many landscape photographs are spoilt because in special conditions the filter layer is not as effective as it should be so that a blue tinge is overlaid on the whole picture.

It must be remembered that since the colours in nature are reproduced in terms of these three primary colours, blue, yellow and red, some loss of colour quality is inevitable, whatever film is used. The colours, whether of a paper print or of a transparency, are, therefore, approximate to those of nature, not identical with them, and the main difference between one film and another is that some over-accentuate blue, others over-accentuate one or other of the remaining primary colours. Some fast films, although much more suitable for simple types of camera, produce pictures of a rather pastel shade which lack the sharp and clear blues, reds and yellows of the slower films.

Because the qualities of daylight and artificial light are different (artificial illumination always has a yellowish tinge) several film manufacturers produce different films for use in daylight and in artificial light.

The relation between the speed of individual films and the exposure to be given is that the faster the film, the less the exposure needed. If film A is twice as fast as film B, then it requires only half the exposure. Alternatively the diaphragm of the camera can be stopped down by one full stop, e.g. from $f/8$ to $f/11$. Colour pictures, negatives or transparencies, which are under-exposed show that the aperture chosen was too small, or the exposure given too little, for the speed of the film used. Similarly, if the finished pictures are over-exposed it shows that the aperture used was too great or the exposure too long.

All films on the market are classified for speed according to several different ratings. Some film packs are labelled with the speed of the film in several scales. Until quite recently most films, whether manufactured in Great Britain or on the Continent, were rated according to the Scheiner scale and this is still sometimes used, though largely obsolescent. The scales now most frequently used are B.S. (British Standards), A.S.A. and DIN. The following conversion table will enable the speed of any film which is quoted on one scale to be converted into another scale:

B.S.	A.S.A.	DIN
21	10	11
22	12	12
23	16	13
24	20	14
25	25	15
26	32	16
27	40	17
28	50	18
29	64	19
30	80	20
31	.00	21
32	125	22
33	160	23

Seven or more types of negative films are available. The list cannot be complete because new films are frequently coming on to the market. No high-speed negative film has yet been produced. Almost all are in the range 25 to 40 A.S.A., that is, between 25° and 27° B.S. There are negative Kodacolor films to fit all cameras taking the popular sizes of roll films—120, 620, 127 and 828. Kodacolor is also supplied in cassettes for 35 mm. cameras. The speed of Kodacolor is 32 A.S.A., or 26° B.S., but it is expected that a faster type of Kodak negative film will soon be available.

Ilfocolor is similar to Kodacolor. Its speed is greater by a small margin and it is possible to take good colour photographs with the most simple type of camera in bright sunshine, providing that the subject to be photographed is directly illuminated by the sun. Results on Ilfocolor with the Sporti and Super Sporti cameras described in the previous chapter, are extremely satisfactory, although when the light cloud or cloudy settings are required the prints are often less pleasing.

In a more versatile camera Ilfocolor gives good results with front lighting, if an exposure of 1/50th of a second and an aperture of $f/11$ is used for most landscapes in bright sunshine and for people on the beach or similarly well lighted positions. When the sunlight is hazy an aperture of $f/8$ and an exposure of 1/50th of a second is satisfactory. When the sun is not shining directly on the subject but the light is good, an aperture of $f/5 \cdot 6$ at 1/50th produces the best results. In dull conditions an aperture of $f/4$ and an exposure of 1/50th is recommended but obviously very precise focusing is necessary if good results are to be produced with such a large aperture.

The drawback is that so many people are unable to hold a camera for as much as 1/50th of a second without movement, however slight, which blurs the sharp outlines of the picture and makes disappointing enlargements. However, it is equally possible to halve the time of the exposure, that is, to use an exposure of 1/100th or 1/125th of a second and increase the aperture correspondingly, i.e. to use an aperture of $f/8$ in bright sunshine, $f/5\cdot6$ in hazy sunshine, $f/4$ in cloudy bright conditions, and avoid taking views when the sky is overcast. Many good photographs, especially of details in buildings or people, can be taken with an aperture of $f/2\cdot8$ or more providing that the focusing is precise, although a range finder, whether built in or not, is almost essential in such cases.

Gevacolor is another reliable film. The negative film is known as N5. It is rather slower than either Ilfocolor or Kodacolor and has a rating of 25 A.S.A. equivalent to the B.S. rating of 25°. Gevacolor is certainly a film which everyone desiring colour prints on paper should try before making a firm decision. It is said that the latitude of Gevacolor is less than that of Ilfocolor or Kodacolor and that therefore a more precise exposure is necessary to produce good results. This, however, is very doubtful, and adequate results can generally be expected if the exposure is not less than half or more than twice the ideal. With this film, as with all the other negative films, pictures can be taken with box cameras only in full sunshine and with the subject directly illuminated by front lighting. With more versatile cameras the manufacturers recommend an aperture of between $f/11$ and $f/16$, with an exposure of 1/50th of a second in full sunshine in summer, for front lighted subjects on the beach or in open country, an aperture between $f/8$ and $f/11$ for most other subjects which are lighted by the sun and do not have any heavy shadows.

The price of Gevacolor is somewhat less than that of the other two types and a similar service for providing enprints $3\frac{1}{2}'' \times 4\frac{1}{2}''$ approximately, is available or, in the case of 12 exposure cameras, $3\frac{1}{2}'' \times 3\frac{1}{2}''$. The drawback of Gevacolor is that the reds are rather insistent compared

with the reds of most other negative films, while the blues
are comparatively muted.

Agfacolor negative films are marketed with two completely different speed ratings. The Agfacolor CN 14 is
available only in 20 exposure cassettes for 35 mm.
cameras, while the Agfacolor CN 17 is available for all
roll film and miniature cameras. The CN 14 film is an
exceptionally slow one with an A.S.A. rating of 20 and a
B.S. rating of 24°. That is the chief reason why it is
recommended only for 35 mm. cameras, which normally
give a greater depth of focus than roll film cameras.

The advantage of CN 14 is its fine grain, more important when enlargements are to be made from 35 mm.
negatives than from negatives of $3\frac{1}{4}'' \times 2\frac{1}{4}''$, or $2\frac{1}{4}'' \times 2\frac{1}{4}''$.
Some sacrifice of quality is usually made for speed, and
there can be little doubt that the CN 14, providing the
correct exposure is given and the focusing is accurate,
produces results, in terms of colour paper prints, as good
as those produced by any other film and better than
many. In spite of the slowness of the film, good pictures
can be taken in most conditions if the camera has an
$f/3\cdot5$ lens or faster. The manufacturers recommend an
exposure of 1/50th of a second with an aperture of $f/11$
for the brightest subjects in clear sunshine, such as open
scenes on the beach, and snow scenes; $f/8$ for similar
scenes in hazy sunshine; $f/6\cdot3$ when the sky is cloudy but
good light is filtering through the clouds; and $f/5\cdot6$ when
the sky is overcast. For normal landscapes the next lower
aperture is recommended, i.e. $f/8$ in clear sunshine,
$f/6\cdot3$ in hazy sun, $f/5\cdot6$ in partly cloudy conditions, and
$f/4\cdot5$ in overcast conditions. For photographing people in
the open, $f/6\cdot3$ is recommended for clear sunshine, $f/5\cdot6$
for hazy sunshine, $f/4\cdot5$ for partly cloudy conditions, and
$f/3\cdot5$ for overcast conditions. Subjects in the shade, even
if the light is brilliant, cannot be photographed satis-

factorily with an aperture of less than $f/5.6$ and an exposure of 1/50th of a second.

The other Agfacolor film, CN 17, is at least twice as fast as the CN 14 with an A.S.A. rating of 40 and a B.S. rating of 27°. This may be regarded as an excellent high-speed film for making negatives, and although rather grainy, its graininess is not apparent on standard en-prints and scarcely visible in enlargements of moderate size.

It is necessary to avoid over-exposure of any Agfacolor film, as the colours have a tendency to be pale if the exposure is only slightly greater than the correct one. Experience suggests that both films are slightly faster in bright sunshine than their rating indicates but latitude is moderate to good and both give fair detail in shadowed areas except in scenes containing particularly bright highlights, or in conditions of exceptionally bright sunshine in which no negative film will give a satisfactory rendering of the highlights and appreciable detail in the shadows.

Adox is a slightly faster negative film. It is available for 120 and 620 cameras, and also for 35 mm. cameras in 20 or 36 exposure cassettes. Clearly this film has certain advantages for the most simple type of camera. It has won many admirers and is thought by many to have slightly greater latitude than other films of comparable speed.

Coronet and Pakolor are two other negative films which many users find give satisfactory results. Both are rated A.S.A. 40, B.S. 27° but neither is available for use in 35 mm. cameras. Coronet is sold in rolls to fit the 120/620 size and also the 127, while Pakolor is only manufactured for the 120/620 size.

The range of reversal films is even greater than that of negative films. Speeds vary from an A.S.A. rating of 10 to, amazingly, one of 160, the equivalent of a fast black and white film. The tendency in recent years, as with negative films, has been towards the production of more and more rapid film, though unhappily without any major increase in versatility or latitude, which appears to be beyond the scope of the hundreds of scientists in many countries who are constantly experimenting with new emulsions. However, there is a reversal film to suit most tastes. The results produced with almost all of them are pleasing, if not exact in colour rendering. As a general rule the faster the film the better it is for the box type or more simple type of 35 mm. camera because with slower films the tendency is to under-exposure unless conditions are really brilliant and the subject being photographed is itself a bright one.

However, it is a case of " each to his choice " and only general guidance can be given. The oldest of all the reversal films, which has been on the market for over 25 years, is Kodachrome. It used to be said that Kodachrome transparencies were " large as life and twice as natural." Certainly the earlier types of Kodachrome rendered blue skies too blue and red features were over-accentuated. Although the general characteristics of the film have not changed since it was the pioneer of colour reversal film, its emulsions have been constantly improved and to-day, if the exposure is correct, its colour rendering is far more exact than it was 10 years ago. Moreover, it is a film almost entirely devoid of grain and therefore ideal for producing transparencies which are intended for projection on a large screen. Its speed rating, however, is only 10 A.S.A., 21° B.S. It is available in 20-exposure or 36-exposure standard cassettes for use in miniature cameras. It is also available in 828 size for the Bantam Colorsnap camera.

Kodachrome film is truly reliable, its only drawback being slowness. In terms of diaphragm settings and exposure values this means that a bright scene in good sunshine, e.g. a beach scene or a distant landscape, requires a setting of $f/6 \cdot 3$ with a shutter speed of 1/50th or

1/60th of a second, while the lens needs to be open to approximately $f/2\cdot8$ in slightly cloudy conditions, thus reducing the depth of field and making precise focusing absolutely essential. For those many people who find it impossible to avoid camera shake with the shutter open more than 1/100th or 1/125th of a second, Kodachrome film is very difficult to use except for limited subjects which admit of precise focusing—a portrait, for instance, or a group on the beach, or in open country—while the rendering of dark subjects in poor lighting conditions is virtually impossible without a complex and expensive camera. Quite an ordinary subject in open shade in summer would require $f/2$ at a shutter speed of 1/100th of a second and such a subject could not be taken either in the early morning or towards sunset, or in winter.

Kodachrome film is processed by the makers. Each roll contains a note of the processing station to which the film has to be sent through the post. Yet in spite of the great pressure upon the processing stations during the holiday season, when probably twenty times as many films are exposed as in late autumn or winter, the results achieved are invariably good—a very great tribute to the skill and care of the staff of the laboratories.

Kodachrome II is a recent addition to the Kodak range of reversal films. It is claimed with complete accuracy to be the product of 25 years of almost continuous experiment. In many ways it sets a new standard while retaining many of the virtues of the original Kodachrome. It is $2\frac{1}{2}$ times as fast as Kodachrome I, with an A.S.A. rating of 25 and a B.S. rating of 25°. The manufacturers claim that it has greater definition and gives improved colour rendering, despite the substantial increase in speed. The indications are that Kodachrome II has as fine a grain as the original Kodachrome, while the colour rendering of the new film allows bright colours and pastel tones to be rendered with greater fidelity. Certainly yellows and greens are more accurate, while reds are without the yellowish tinge which marred many transparencies taken from the earlier Kodachrome film. There is also lower contrast, which improves the exposure latitude and enables a greater degree of detail in shadow areas, while not grossly over-exposing the highlights. As with the original Kodachrome, processing is carried out by the manufacturers and the cost of processing is included in the price of the film.

Satisfactory supplies of Kodachrome II for most cameras have become available in the British market. 20 exposure cassettes for 35 mm. cameras have been obtainable for some time and these have been followed by 36 exposure cassettes and 12 exposure rolls for 828 cameras. Although the price is slightly higher than that of Kodachrome I, the difference works out at rather less than a penny for each transparency. The declared intention of the manufacturers is to allow Kodachrome I and II to be available side by side, but it is a fair inference that before long Kodachrome I will disappear from the shops, if only because the demand for it will cease.

Experiments carried out for the American journal *Modern Photography* show that many of the claims made for Kodachrome II are justified, especially its greater latitude compared with the earlier type, giving more detail in shadows and permitting a reasonable transparency to be made even if the exposure is not strictly accurate.

These detailed tests suggest that Kodachrome II in many conditions is more than two and a half times as fast as I. This is especially true in the case of subjects evenly lit by sunshine with no large areas of shadow. In such cases the A.S.A. rating appears to the American experts to be nearer 40 than 25, though the reading of 25 is perfectly satisfactory as a compromise where shadows and highlights appear in the same subject. Even so, an under-exposed shadow area is preferable to an over-exposed highlight area, in which the colours are almost completely washed out.

There is no doubt, either, that the grain of Kodachrome II is as fine as that of I and although this has little significance in normal projection of transparencies on a good screen, it is very important if major enlargements are required either as transparencies or paper prints. The finer grain might also be important if large-size projections are required for a lecture hall.

The greater latitude of the new film is an advantage, while the higher speed will allow a much greater depth of field in sharp focus with the same shutter speed. It has also been demonstrated that portraits, whether taken outdoors or indoors, show a better rendering of skin tones with the new film, or at any rate give a more natural effect. Unhappily, the most natural rendering of skin tones is not always preferred by the person being photographed!

An extensive range of subjects photographed by the American experts showed that the greater latitude of the new film assured a more natural rendering of blues, particularly the blues of sea and sky, and a far better reproduction of lightly shadowed areas. The only drawback of the new film is that its comparative lack of contrast makes dramatic subjects, such as a stormy sky, less impressive, even though the detail and colour rendering of the foreground is much better. There is also the reservation that though the new film gives greater detail in shadowed areas, its rendering of shadows without detail is less satisfactory than that of the earlier film, with a greyish tinge in place of the luminous black of Kodachrome I. It was found, too, that although the rendering of colour values with normal exposure was vastly superior, over-exposure of the new film resulted in less differentiation of greens, blues, and yellows compared with Kodachrome I, though red and darker yellow tints were about equal.

It is impossible to be dogmatic, but in all probability the higher speed and other advantages of Kodachrome II will outweigh the virtues of the earlier film and will make it more popular. Kodachrome II may even supersede Ektachrome, which has been on the market for some years, and, unlike Kodachrome, can be developed by the amateur. The speed of Ektachrome is A.S.A. 32, B.S. 26°. It is available for most roll film cameras and also for 35 mm. cameras. When it was first introduced into America it was hailed as the reversal film of the future and was used by film companies and professional photographers for producing large-size colour transparencies. It is in every way a fully satisfactory and reliable film, though it has rather more grain than Kodachrome I and II.

Most remarkable of all the reversal films in the Kodak range is Ektachrome HS (high speed), which has an A.S.A. rating of 160 and a B.S. rating of 33°. It is said to be the world's fastest colour film and makes it possible to take photographs in dull conditions in the depth of winter with any camera having a lens of $f/3·5$ or better. One can indeed treat Ektachrome HS in exactly the same way as one would treat high-speed monochrome film. It is a great triumph to have produced such a high-speed film for colour photography. Its only drawback is that the primary colours are not so brightly rendered as on slower speed film, although the exposure latitude is excellent. It is possible, for instance, to take a normally lighted subject on a cloudy day in winter with a shutter speed of 1/50th or 1/60th of a second, and an aperture between $f/3·5$ and $f/4·5$, while in bright summer sunshine correct rendering of colours in an open landscape can be obtained with a shutter speed of 1/100th to 1/125th of a second at $f/16$.

Many indoor shots in colour, only possible before with the aid of flash lighting can be undertaken in available daylight using a hand-held camera with HS Ektachrome film. The film also makes it possible to photograph swiftly moving objects in a greater variety of lighting conditions than any other. Many professional photographers use it at race meetings, athletic events, air shows, and the like. HS Ektachrome is also exceptional in its rendering of white, and is especially useful with a telephoto lens. Although 160 A.S.A. is by any standard of comparison a fast film, the speed of Ektachrome HS can be doubled by increasing the processing time in the first developer by three minutes. This increase of time in processing does not affect the balance of the colour values, but it does result inevitably in an increase in the graininess of the transparency and can only be recommended if photographs have been taken which it would not have been practical to take without a film speed of 300 A.S.A. or more.

Ilfochrome is the universal film in the Ilford range. It has a speed rating of A.S.A. 32, B.S. 26°. It has a very fine grain, finer indeed than the original Ilfochrome, which was rated as A.S.A. 10, B.S. 21° and which it replaces. Its colour rendering is bold, its latitude good, but perhaps not so great as that of some faster films. It has the same capacity as Kodachrome for rendering shadow areas in a convincing tone. Its higher speed compared with the original Ilfachrome makes it better suited for use in simple types of camera or box cameras with fixed focus and fixed aperture. An exposure of 1/100th of a second between $f/6\cdot3$ and $f/8$ can be recommended for average subjects front lit by bright sunshine, of 1/50th of a second with the same aperture for subjects photographed in hazy sunshine, and 1/50th of a second at $f/4\cdot5$ for average subjects when the sky is slightly overcast. In dull weather an exposure of 1/25th at $f/3\cdot5$ is recommended, but it must be remembered that 1/25th is a comparatively long exposure and unless the shutter is released with extreme care and while the breath is being held, some camera shake is almost inevitable, however slight—enough at any rate to blur the outlines of a 35 mm. transparency projected on to a large screen. Moreover, the makers recommend that these exposures should be used only between three hours after sunrise and three hours before sunset.

For very light subjects with no dark areas a lens aperture half to one stop smaller than that indicated should be used, while for dark subjects with no important highlights an aperture half to one stop larger is advised. Similarly, a lens aperture at least one stop larger must be used for photographs taken within two hours after sunrise and two hours before sunset. But in these conditions results are often disappointing owing to the difference between the quality of sunlight in the early morning and late evening, compared with that in the middle of the day. However, all this is equally true of Kodachrome and there is probably not a great deal to choose between the two, although individual users will prefer the colour rendering of one to the other.

Ilford Ltd. provide a service similar to that offered by Kodak Ltd. for making paper prints in colour from 24 mm. × 36 mm. transparencies, that is, from the usual size of transparency obtained from a 35 mm. camera. Prints are made in two standard sizes—$3\frac{3}{4}'' \times 5\frac{1}{2}''$ and $5\frac{1}{2}'' \times 8\frac{1}{4}''$. If the transparencies are smaller than 24 mm. × 36 mm. the sizes of the prints are in proportion. The cost of the smaller print is approximately 2/6, with a minimum order of four, of the larger print approximately 7/6 with no minimum order demanded. These prices are subject to variation, like all prices of photographic services and equipment, but with the vast increase in the popularity of colour the tendency, apart from any budgetary increases, is downwards.

Ferraniacolor, an Italian film, is slower than Ilfochrome but unlike Kodachrome and Ilfochrome can be developed with a home processing kit. It is claimed also that Ferraniacolor is more simple to process at home than any other reversal film. Its speed is 25 A.S.A., 25° B.S. This permits an exposure of 1/100th of a second at $f/8$ for front lit subjects in bright sunshine, when the colours of the subject are predominantly light, or of 1/100th at $f/6.5$ for average subjects. Even dark subjects in cloudy weather can be photographed with this film at 1/50th of a second at $f/4$. Allowance must be made, as with all other reversal films, for the season and for the time of day. In winter a larger aperture or a longer exposure is essential. Similarly, an allowance of half a stop at least must be made for subjects to be photographed within two or three hours of sunrise or sunset.

Ferraniacolor, like Kodachrome, is entirely reliable and its rendering of colours is at least as satisfactory as that of the other films described. Films of this medium speed are often preferred by professional as well as amateur photographers to the slower films, or the very fast films such as Ektachrome HS. The reason is that the primary colours appear brighter than those rendered by very high-speed films but not quite so bright as those rendered by slower films. The balance between blues, reds, and yellows is very delicate, but one might say that given the correct exposure the balance in Ferraniacolor is as good as that given by any film, though in landscapes in clear sunshine the blue of the sky is often rather too intense.

Gevacolor R5, a Belgian film, is much faster, with a rating of 40 A.S.A. and 27° B.S. This again at the present state of research into emulsions must be regarded as a medium-speed film. It is slightly cheaper (the processing price is included in the price of the film) than most of the English films and has very much the same qualities as Ferraniacolor. Its rendering of colours is pleasing and it is particularly suited to seascapes on clear days, because the rendering of the blue of the sea is not too bright. Its reds, too, are above criticism and rarely show any of the yellowish tinge which mars the reds rendered by some reversal films. The exposures and apertures necessary are similar to those recommended for Ferraniacolor, the allowance for the extra speed being about a full stop, but the advantage of this appreciably faster film is that it is well adapted to take pictures with a simple camera in average lighting conditions.

Three German films deserve special mention—Adox, Perutz and Agfacolor. All have precisely the same speed rating—50 A.S.A., 28° B.S. Agfacolor has been available in Great Britain for some years, Adox and Perutz are relative newcomers, but all have their special virtues. Agfacolor is supplied for all popular sizes of roll films and in 20 and 36 exposure cassettes for 35 mm. cameras; Perutz in 20 and 36 exposure cassettes for 35 mm. cameras; and Adox in 15 and 36 exposure cassettes for 35 mm. cameras. In each case the cost of processing is included in the price of the film, the price of Perutz being slightly lower than that of the other two. Perutz and Adox must be returned to Germany for processing.

All three films give excellent results. A criticism often made of Agfacolor is that its colours are more pastel than they appear in nature but this is largely a fault of inaccurate exposure. The blues rendered by Perutz film are completely natural, making it very satisfactory for the ever-popular seaside photographs, but the greens are rather darker than in nature when the exposure recommended by the manufacturer is given. If the exposure is increased so as to lighten the green, the blues of sea and sky tend to look rather washed out. All three permit the use of a shutter speed of 1/100th to 1/125th of a second with an aperture of $f/11$ for open scenes in bright summer sunshine. Moreover the speed of these films makes it entirely practical to take shaded subjects in hazy or even cloudy conditions with a shutter speed of 1/100th to 1/125th of a second and an aperture of between $f/2\cdot8$ and $f/4$, well within the range of the many medium-priced cameras, such as the Werra.

Kranzcolor C 18 is the newest of the reversal films. At present it is obtainable only through one chain of photographic dealers. Its speed is identical with that of the other German films which have been mentioned. Its great attraction is that its price, including processing, is between 20 and 30 per cent less than that of any other film on the market. Does one lose anything with the cheaper film? Experience suggests that, like every other film, Kranzcolor has its advantages and its drawbacks and that the over-all loss comparable with films of similar speed is negligible. Transparencies taken from 36 exposure cassettes for 35 mm. cameras cost under 10d. each at the present price. In addition transparencies are returned from Germany already mounted.

All the films reviewed above are specially designed for photography out of doors. Some manufacturers market films designed specifically for photography by artificial light in view of the fact that the colour of artificial light is materially different from that of sunlight. These special indoor films will be mentioned in the chapter on Photographing Indoors.

CHAPTER 3

Taking a Good Colour Photograph

The choice of the right camera and the right film, having regard to the kind of photographs it is proposed to take and the cost of the equipment, as described in the previous two chapters, is more than half the effort required to achieve good photographs in colour. Other necessary equipment is relatively insignificant but there are one or two inexpensive exceptions to this rule. The first and the most important is a lens hood. Some cameras, like the Werra, are sold with a built-in lens hood. In the majority of cameras, however, it is an inexpensive and worthwhile extra which must be purchased separately.

The use of a lens hood is even more important when working in colour than in monochrome. Many amateurs with long experience of black and white photography do not bother to fit a hood unless they are photographing against the sun. Purists deplore this tendency but with front or side lighting the difference in rendering subjects in black and white, with or without a hood, is not great enough to spoil the picture. The case is very different in colour, for it is essential that the only light reaching the lens should be that reflected by the subject being photographed. Without a lens hood, even with direct lighting, the whole balance of a picture may be upset by light from above or from the side, especially blue light from the sky or sea. In sunny weather the amount of blue light emanating from the sky is always troublesome but its effect is minimised by the use of a hood.

A range-finder and exposure meter are often regarded

as essential. As already mentioned, many of the more expensive cameras are fitted with built-in range-finders and exposure meters, but the majority of cameras in use to-day have neither. With the simplest form of cameras which have a fixed focus, a fixed aperture, and a fixed shutter speed, neither is of the slightest use, but even with inexpensive cameras which have variable shutter speeds, variable apertures, and focusing devices, both can be very useful. With the more expensive types of camera not fitted with a coupled range-finder or meter but with a high quality lens, shutter, and focusing scale ranging from a few feet to infinity, both become almost essential.

A range-finder enables the photographer to focus the lens on the part of the subject which he considers most important. If a picture is being taken of a person or a group, it is essential that the subject should be in the sharpest possible focus. The background does not matter. Indeed a blurred or indefinite background is often an advantage, but a picture in which the person or group is out of focus is always a failure.

One can dispense with a range-finder by using a tape measure, or, less certainly, by pacing out the distance between the camera and the subject, the usual measure of distance being one stride to one yard. Neither of these methods is satisfactory. Measuring with a tape takes too long and makes a human subject nervous and self-consci-ous. Measuring by strides is quite inaccurate, if only because the strides of different people vary considerably. A reliable range-finder can be bought for less than two pounds and the transference of the distance as measured by the range-finder to the focusing ring of the camera is a matter of seconds.

This does not imply that every subject calls for the use of a range-finder. Any subject which is more than 75 feet from the photographer can safely be photographed on infinity, one between 30 and 75 feet at a little less than infinity or on 48 feet which is a distance usually marked on the focusing ring. For subjects between 20 and 30 feet from the camera a setting at 24 feet may be used and with an aperture of $f/8$ or smaller, clear definition will be obtained from about 10 feet to infinity with a miniature camera. Even so, the human eye is fallible in judging distances and a range-finder will help to correct this.

Exposure meters are in a rather different category. Many models are on the market. It may be assumed that any one which is recommended by a photographic dealer is efficient in its own way. The simple " extinction " type, however, is not really suitable for colour photography because the readings which it gives are not sufficiently precise. The photo-electric meter is always precise and it is this type which is generally built into the more expensive types of camera, such as the Rolleiflex.

Even so, the finest type of meter, such as the Weston, should be used with discretion, for it is essential to point it precisely at what is being photographed in order to obtain an accurate reading rather than, as many beginners do, direct it vaguely in the direction of the subject, when it gives a reading corresponding to that of the scene as a whole (influenced by the brightness of the sky) rather than that of the focus of interest. It is a good rule always to point the meter slightly downwards.

If a group of people is being photographed on the beach or in the country under a blue sky, it is not sufficient to point the exposure meter in the general direction of the group, take a reading from it, and transfer it to the camera. It is essential to take the meter near the group and point it at individual members. The reading will then be influenced by the colour of the clothes worn by each member of the group. The correct exposure will be determined by taking an average of these readings.

Experience is necessary to use a meter with advantage. For photographers with no experience, the exposure tables included with most rolls or cassettes of colour film may well prove more reliable guides. But these exposure tables can only take account of average conditions, as all manufacturers admit, so that the experienced user of a meter is in a much better position to judge the correct exposure. When it is remembered that the latitude of most colour films to secure the best possible rendering of colour is less than one stop, it will be appreciated that this assistance in determining the best aperture and exposure is most valuable.

Incorrect exposures may result even with a meter since this can only give an average reading for the whole scene if used from the camera position. When a reading is taken on a very light subject without many shadows the result is not accurate, nor is the reading any more satisfactory for a dark subject without highlights. For this reason it is often recommended that for best results (in terms of exposure) the " highlight " method should be used, by taking what is known as an incident light reading. Some exposure meters have an incident light attachment, the reading being taken of the light falling on the subject instead of the light reflected by it. It is certainly true that exposures calculated from the results of reflected light reading can be very misleading. When the exposure meter is built into the camera it may not be practical to obtain an incident light reading. That is the reason why it has been stressed in this book that even the most precise light meter must be used with discretion.

Filters are a major pre-occupation with photographers in monochrome, whether amateur or professional. Their purpose is to render colours in black and white as nearly as possible in conformity with their relative brightness in nature. No such problem arises with colour photography.

All the negative and reversal films at present on the market are designed to render colours as nearly as possible according to nature without the use of filters. Some conversion filters are provided for making films designed for photographing in the open air suitable for indoor photography and these will be mentioned in a later chapter.

For outdoor photography, however, the only filter which need be considered is the ultra violet one. An ultra violet (U.V.) filter absorbs some of the blue light in the atmosphere and has the great merit of not requiring an increased exposure. Photographers differ considerably in their estimate of the value of U.V. filters. Some people use one always, because the majority of films render blue rather brighter than it appears to the human eye. But its use with ordinary subjects in normal lighting conditions reduces the " punch " of the print or transparency. It is far better to reserve its use for subjects in which blue light is particularly insistent. Such subjects include beach scenes dominated by a blue sky and reflected by the sea, and especially landscapes photographed under a blue sky or at high altitudes, where haze is virtually non-existent and the blue of the sky is the dominating colour factor. A U.V. filter is also useful during high summer in weather conditions such as are generally encountered in June, July and August in the Mediterranean countries.

Surprisingly to most beginners, a blue cast appears in shadowed subjects lit by a blue sky even in temperate climates, and still more often when the sky is cloudy. This cast can be corrected to some extent by the use of a U.V. filter, but experience alone can show when its use is valuable. However, the suggestions given above should prove an adequate foundation on which to base this experience.

The only other accessory which can be recommended for successful photography in colour is a tripod. Tripods like light meters are sometimes a drawback. If a tripod is to be used it is vital that it should be rigid enough, if used in the open air, not to be swayed in the slightest degree by wind and not to be moved by the action of releasing the shutter. Generally speaking, hand-held exposures are best, if only because they alone can catch the spirit of a spontaneous action, especially when people are being photographed. By the time one has set up a tripod, screwed in the camera, focused, and released the shutter, any spontaneity in a scene involving people is inevitably lost. A tripod is, however, extremely useful when photographing buildings in poor light, when an exposure of more than 1/50th of a second is necessary, and absolutely essential when photographing indoors with available light, as when photographing stained glass windows by the light filtering into a church, when an exposure of several seconds may be indicated. Its use is not advised when photographing landscapes. If the light is not sufficiently good to permit a short exposure with a hand-held camera the colours of the scene are unlikely to be worth recording. One might say that for colour photography a tripod is a necessary part of the equipment of a professional who must be prepared to take pictures in any lighting conditions, rather than of the amateur, who can choose his subject and photograph it when the light is suitable.

Granted that the equipment has been wisely chosen, there is no reason why a beginner should not take good photographs in colour. Many hold the view that colour is a simpler medium than black and white and flatters the beginner. To some extent at least, this is true, because if the exposure given to the subject is within the range of tolerance of the film, the colour rendering is more attractive than a monochrome rendering to the ordinary person who is not a photographic enthusiast and wants only a representation of people and places which have some special association. Although in theory an unrelieved foreground in one colour is just as bad as a vast expanse of grey in the foreground of a monochrome photograph, in practice the rendering of a dull foreground in colour, whether as a colour print or a transparency, looks much better than its monochrome equivalent.

The first rule, then, for everyone who has not previously worked in colour is not to be afraid of the medium but to photograph with complete confidence that the result may be interesting or evocative of happy memories, even though the photograph is not good by technical standards. The second is to discover by experience precisely what is the capacity of one's camera and film. This is of the utmost importance because, as any photographic printer will agree, far more photographs are ruined because they were exposed in totally unsuitable conditions of light than for any other fault on the part of the photographer.

Experience is the only guide to the capacity of a particular type of film. That is one of the reasons why it is best to make one's choice of film, and after the choice is made, use the same film whenever possible. It is futile to be discouraged if one or two rolls or cassettes produce imperfect results. Studying them carefully will show the way to better results and these better results will assuredly follow, providing one is not discouraged by initial setbacks.

It must be stressed here that for simple cameras, and especially the box type with fixed aperture and shutter, the negative colour films have one great advantage over reversal films. The acceptable error in exposure, that is to say, the deviation from the correct exposure (and there is always one single correct exposure for every subject in every lighting condition) is less than a stop in the case of reversal films. If the correct setting is $f/8$ at 1/50th of a second the resulting transparency is unlikely to be a pleasing one if the aperture used is as small as $f/11$ or as large as

57

$f/5\cdot6$. This fact presents a major difficulty in using cameras priced under about £10. The position in regard to negative films is different. Although negative films are generally slower than the most modern types of reversal film, they permit of a much greater error in exposure. In this respect they are similar to black and white films. A negative is produced and the result depends on the skill of the printer.

The possibility of correcting exposure faults on a transparency is slight, but the standard even of commercial printing in colour from negatives is extremely high, especially if it is done outside the period of holiday congestion. The makers recommend that all colour films should be processed as soon as possible, but it is quite sound advice to retain a roll exposed in August until September, when the pressure on the processers is less. The fact remains that with skilful printing pleasing colour prints can be obtained from negatives even if the negatives are considerably under- or over-exposed. If the correct exposure is $f/8$ at 1/50th of a second, adequate prints are possible if the photograph is taken with an aperture of $f/11$ or $f/5\cdot6$.

Some people find difficulty in distinguishing between correctly exposed and under- or over-exposed transparencies, yet it is essential to be able to identify a fault of this kind which can be corrected. An under-exposed transparency shows colours darker than they appear in nature while the shadow areas contain no detail. In an over-exposed transparency the colours are pale or "washed out." The fact that detail is good in the shadow areas is no real compensation for the pale and anaemic appearance of the highlights. With a correct exposure the colours appear much as in real life, though the blues are always, or almost always, rather brighter. Although ideally there should be some slight detail in the shadow areas in exceptionally bright sunshine with front lighting, it is hopeless to expect correct rendering of the highlights and full detail in the shadows. That is why so many authorities recommend that transparencies should not be attempted of subjects which have extensive areas of shadow and bright highlights.

While speaking of shadows and highlights, it is timely to make an important reservation to generally accepted practice. It is nearly always said that inexperienced photographers should confine themselves to subjects which are lighted directly by bright sunshine, the sun being behind the photographer. That is admittedly a good rule when using the most simple type of camera. But it is equally true that most outstanding colour photographs are taken when the sun is not unduly bright, providing that the camera is versatile enough for the correct exposure to be made in the available light. With a hazy sun there is far less contrast between highlights and shadows and, therefore, far less risk of some parts of the picture being grossly over-exposed, while other parts are equally under-exposed.

Different subjects demand very different lighting conditions and this point will emerge in the following chapters which deal with particular types of photographs. It must always be remembered that although front lighting is inevitably the best for the cheapest cameras, especially if a slow film is being used, it is only the best because it is the only possible light with which photographs can be taken. In general, hazy sunshine is to be preferred pictorially to sunshine with a dark blue sky, while side lighting in suitable conditions enhances the apparent depth of the picture and often gives a much more exciting rendering than front lighting. Even back lighting can produce magnificent transparencies just as it often renders fine monochrome pictures.

There is no reason why an amateur should not experiment with side and back lighting once he has mastered the capabilities of his camera and his film, provided that he is using a camera which will enable correctly exposed pictures to be taken in these conditions. In brief, there is no mystery about photographing in colour. It is just as simple a process as photographing in monochrome and for most people infinitely more rewarding. But photography is an art in the same way as sketching or painting, even though the actual taking of photographs is mechanical: time and experience are necessary for it to be mastered. Like every other art, its finest expression depends to some extent on the flair or genius of the photographer. But as most of us take photographs for our own pleasure and that of a few of our friends or family, the degree of skill and knowledge necessary for acceptable results to be obtained is a matter for our own judgment. It is defeatist to transform one of the finest of all hobbies into hard labour, or to concentrate on scientific excellence when the aim is to produce record photographs for the enjoyment of a limited number of people.

What, then, does make a good picture? Scores of books have been written about the principles of composition in monochrome and in colour—and the two are quite different. But it is very, very doubtful whether composition can be reduced to exact principles definable in words. One has a great deal of sympathy with the eminent photographer who described treatises on composition as highfalutin' nonsense. What we set out to do is to produce a pleasing picture. Very many people have an instinctive awareness of what makes a good picture, or at least a good picture in their own eyes, which is the important thing. In the following chapters a good deal will be said about ways and means of photographing subjects which present special difficulties. What will be said in this chapter amounts only to general advice, based on experience, for producing colour prints or transparencies which appear pleasing to most people.

One of the most important rules in composing a picture is simplicity. Indeed, a good picture may be defined as one in which the various parts which compose it are arranged in such a way that the effect is harmonious, and this harmony can only be achieved if the arrangement is simple. If one takes a number of vases of flowers and puts them all together on one table, the effect is unlikely to be pleasing to the eye unless the flowers are very carefully chosen. Arrange them on several tables or around the room and the effect is one of beauty which gives pleasure to all who see it. The same is true in arranging the subject of a photograph. The photographer has a slightly more difficult task than the flower arranger but the principle is the same. In most cases the photographer must cope with the arrangement which nature has ordered. Nature enters into almost every snapshot which the amateur is likely to take, but a great deal can be done to modify any view or the aspect of any building, even of groups of people, by changing the angle of photography.

Another basic rule of composition is that the photograph must have unity given by a single dominant feature. It makes no difference what one is photographing. If the photograph is of a building, then that building must be pictured in such a way that it stands out from its surroundings, and above all, that it is not dominated by them. If the photograph is a landscape, then some special feature in the landscape must be chosen as the centre of interest. If people are the subject of the photograph, then they must be made to stand out. As we shall see later, there are many ways of doing this, but once one has grasped the principle the ways of giving effect to it become very nearly a matter of intuition. It is not so much a matter of working out precisely the angle of photography or of eliminating deliberately objects which conflict with the main subject of interest, as of choosing quite spontaneously the best angle from which the photograph can be taken and the best way of dealing with the background.

One way of focusing interest on the main subject much used by photographers in black and white, but equally useful in colour, is to frame the picture, under an arch, for instance, or between trees, or merely by so arranging the picture that the left and right edges are occupied by fairly dark but not over-emphasised subjects. One example will indicate what is meant. If the subject to be photographed is an inn, unity can often be given to the picture by including the inn sign on one side of the photograph, so preventing the eye from wandering away from the main subject of interest.

Depth can be suggested by receding lines carrying the eye from the foreground to the background, but this device is really only needed when long shots are being taken. The receding lines may be provided by hedges or a road in a landscape, or a line of groins on the beach, but the same three-dimensional effect can be given by making sure that there is a feature of interest in the foreground, the middle distance and the background.

The most important difference between composing in colour and in black and white is that the monochrome photographer has to think in terms of black, white and greys and the way in which his film will render the colours of nature in this medium, whereas the photographer in colour need not concern himself with this, since he can see the picture before him in approximately the same colours as it will be reproduced. His main preoccupation is with contrasting masses of colour. Many of the best colour photographs are those in which the centre of interest is in a bright colour, the surroundings in more pastel shades. The dominance of red must never be overlooked. Even a small area of red provides a dramatic highlight and redeems many otherwise dull or featureless scenes.

A great deal is heard of the contrast between warm colours and cold colours and the ways in which these can be combined to produce a pleasing picture. It is probably unwise for the beginner to concern himself too closely with these except to remember that blue is a cold colour, red a warm one, and yellow and green are intermediate between red and blue. But it is wholly a matter of taste whether a picture of predominantly warm tints is preferred to one of predominantly cold tints. The great German photographer, Walther Benser, who has given lectures illustrated with colour slides in almost every country of Europe, has said that he has found that warm-hued pictures are preferred by Scandinavian peoples and by most people of Northern Europe, whereas pictures of predominantly cold tints are preferred by the people of Italy, southern France, and Spain. That is only another way of saying that most people like to see something to which they are not accustomed. The warm tints conjure up the thoughts of holidays in hot sunshine for northern people, the cool tints bring to the minds of southerners the thought of snow-clad mountains and ice-covered lakes.

Similarly it is a matter of taste whether the over-accented colours of Kodachrome, for instance, or the more muted colours of Agfacolor are preferred. On the one hand there is a great deal to be said for the " glorious techni-color " effect of the bright colours when slides are pro-jected in a darkened room; on the other, there is much to be said for the more muted colours which are usually nearer to nature, when slides are seen in a viewer. This point is seldom recognised but is very important. Colours cannot be exactly defined and people are notoriously bad at remembering them. This is no doubt partly because the same object appears to have quite different shades of colour in different lights. In a darkened room, when slides are being projected on to a screen, the eye accepts the colours as they are projected because there is no standard of comparison as there generally is when a viewer is being used and the eye tends to reject them as being different from those of nature. Moreover, perception of colour varies enormously from person to person. " Colour blindness " varies from a complete inability to distinguish one colour from another to a difficulty in assessing differences between colours which are very near to each other in the spectrum.

The lesson to be learned from this is that one should never be discouraged if the colours reproduced are not strictly in conformity with the colours of nature as they were seen when the photograph was taken. The effect produced when they are projected may be entirely pleasing. Moreover, most negative films are designed to produce prints whose colours will approximate to those in nature when viewed in daylight. They will look quite different when seen by artificial light. Similarly, a number of reversal films are designed to produce transparencies which will be projected on to a white screen in a darkened room. If one views them, as so many people do, by holding them up to the sky or a bright artificial light, their effect will be different.

Although the manufacturers of most reversal films advise that exposure should not be made two or three hours after sunrise and two or three hours before sunset, those who prefer pictures of a warm tint find that some of their best results are obtained in the two hours before sunset, although a longer exposure must be given to off-set the decrease in the brightness of the light. By contrast, those who prefer cold colours will find that many of their happiest pictures are taken in cloudy conditions, when a bluish tinge tends to be superimposed on all the colours

The historic buildings of England and many other countries provide as good subjects for colour as for black and white photography, but the success of the picture above is achieved with the help of the blue river, the pink blossom, the white swans, and the green bushes setting off the graceful lines and muted colours of Pulteney Bridge in Bath. *Kodak Kodachrome film.*

The High Street, Oxford, always known as "The High", is the perfect subject for the photographer in search of old buildings. This kind of subject is made much easier to picture if a wide-angle lens is used. *Kodak Ektachrome film.*

depicted, or in conditions in which blue is the predominant colour as, for instance, a seascape or beach scene under a dark blue sky. As we have seen, the bluish tinge can be reduced by the use of a U.V. filter, but there are a number of people to whom this appears not as an element spoiling the picture but rather as one enhancing its attraction.

CHAPTER 4

Photographing People

It is always difficult to apply general rules to particular cases. All that has been said so far is directly applicable to the photographing of people in colour, individuals or groups, in any circumstances. Yet every individual picture of people presents a special problem. It is unfortunate, perhaps, that a very high proportion of the photographs taken by beginners are of people but it is perfectly natural that they should want above all to picture their children, their husbands, or wives, and the friends they make on holiday. It is easy with even the simplest cameras, given the right conditions, to take a photograph which will bring back memories of a happy holiday, the bright skies and warm sun, and the charming people one has met. But it is possible with only a little trouble to achieve much more than a mere record photograph.

The real essential of a picture of people—and this applies also to monochrome—is that the people should not be self-conscious, that is, that they should not be aware that they are being photographed at the time the exposure is made. All posed groups look wooden or static. Almost all portraits unless handled by an experienced professional are failures. Many professional photographs are unsatisfactory, however great the trouble and care given by the photographer. One can prove the truth of this by showing the resulting photographs to the subject. When they are posed deliberately the comment nearly always is " Do I really look as ugly as that? " The comment is often a sound one, because people when they have prepared themselves to be photographed and have assumed what they believe to be a photogenic position show no animation or character. The photograph, whether it is in black and white or in colour, lacks movement, one of the essentials of a good photograph.

The first rule in photographing people is to take them unawares. Even if they know they are being photographed one must try to take the photograph at a moment when their interest is distracted.

The second rule is to photograph them doing something, because this gives the impression of movement and is especially important in colour photographs. It does not matter in the least what they are doing. They may be paddling on the beach or lighting a pipe, or merely walking across the area contained within the photographic frame. Whatever they are doing, the act of movement obviates the static character which ruins so many photographs of people.

Lighting is of supreme importance and presents a real problem to photographers who are equipped with simple cameras. One cannot neglect the advice of the film manufacturers, implied by the aperture and exposure recommended by them, that a given film is most suitable for taking photographs with front lighting in bright sunshine, but front lighting with a blue sky and the sun shining straight down on the subject is far from ideal. It is impossible to face the sun without squinting. Many people wear dark glasses in bright sun, but it is doubtful whether a colour photograph which shows the subject in dark glasses can ever be pleasing. Moreover a high sun throws ugly shadows over the face—shadows of the nose and the eyebrows which obscure the eyes and that cast by a woman's hair across the forehead. If the exposure is right for the highlights these shadows must be black unless special equipment is used and the result is anything but happy. That is why so few people who are photographed in colour find the likeness flattering.

There are two ways of overcoming these difficulties. The first and easiest way for the user of a simple camera is to load it with negative film, which gives much greater latitude and permits some control in making the finished print. The second is to load the camera with one of the fast reversal films so that properly exposed photographs are possible when the sun is not shining out of a clear blue sky. For photographing people or groups of people there is no doubt that a hazy sun is to be preferred to a bright sun. Even with front lighting in such conditions, the subject does not inevitably squint, while there are none of the ugly shadows on the face and body associated with bright sunlight.

Although close-ups are usually more pleasing than any other kind of photograph of people, the user of a simple camera will be well advised to take the photograph at a distance of at least 12 feet from the subject. Those who are fortunate enough to possess a more versatile instrument with varied shutter speeds and a satisfactory focusing device can do far more to make attractive pictures of people. Close-up shots become relatively easy and there is no difficulty in achieving adequate light for a good photograph. The only sound advice that can be given is, " never take a photograph of people in the brightest of light unless it is essential to do so." Hazy sunshine will provide the best light, but cloudy conditions, if the person being photographed is gaily dressed or there are other bright colours in the picture, will often yield excellent results.

The main difficulty is the blue cast which mars so many pictures taken in cloudy or dull conditions. The solution to this difficulty is the use of a U.V. filter. Direct front lighting is unnecessary and side lighting is much to be preferred if the lens, shutter, and film speed permit of it without under-exposure. One can even think in terms of photographs taken against the light, which are often most attractive if the shadowed areas, that is, the face and body of the subject, show sufficient detail.

The rendering of skin tones in colour is another problem which can be overcome in part by various simple devices. First, it must be remembered that different films will give different renderings of skin tones in different lights. As only one rendering can be strictly accurate, it follows that the skin colours of people photographed even in the best conditions only approximate to those of nature. We are much more sensitive to errors in rendering skin tones than to similar errors in rendering landscape colours, chiefly because we have a standard of comparison ready to hand. We forget the gradations in the colours of a country scene or of a building. We are much less likely to forget the characteristic colouring of an individual or even of a group of people. Because this rendering of the precise colouring of people's skin, or for that matter even of the lipstick which individual girls use, is such a variable factor, it is far wiser for the beginner to photograph people in gaily coloured clothes which form an integral part of the print or the transparency rather than to concentrate on the face or the body. Another way of expressing this truth is that a pretty girl on the beach is much more likely to be flattered by a photograph taken of her dressed in a gaily coloured playsuit, or wrapped around by bright-coloured towelling, than she is by one of her dressed in a bikini.

Portraiture is a highly specialised form of photography which many experienced professionals find difficult. How much more difficult is it, then, for the amateur who may have to guess the correct exposure or whose experience is not varied enough to allow him to interpret the readings even of a first-class electric exposure meter. Moreover the difficulties of portraiture in colour are far greater than in black and white.

Something now must be said about the quality of light if good pictures of people are to be taken. The nature of light varies greatly. There is the obvious difference between the light of a sunny day and of a cloudy day, but also the less obvious difference between the light at midday and that in the early morning or late afternoon within an hour or two of sunrise and sunset. The midday sun in summer gives a harsh white light, the late evening sun gives a warm, relatively red light. These differences are faithfully portrayed by colour film, even though our eyes tend to neglect them. The effect is to make people look unduly sun-burnt in the evening, unduly pale at midday. All films are slightly different in their sensitivity to light. But once more, experience is the only guide to the best time for portraits.

The rendering of skin tones is affected considerably by the colour of the surroundings. Blue sea and blue sky will result in a blue cast over the skin, capable of only partial correction by a U.V. filter. Glaring white sand will make people look pale. Surrounding woodlands, if the sun is very bright and the reflected light considerable, will cast a most unflattering greenish tinge on faces. In brief, we have to remember that light is reflected by bright objects on to nearby figures and this reflected light determines the rendering of the skin tones.

It has already been said that photographs of people taken with back lighting are often more effective than those taken with front lighting. The problem is to introduce sufficient detail into the shadowed areas of the figures. All that the sun will do is to make pleasing highlights of colour on the hair and around the shoulders of the subject, or, if it is a full-length study, to outline the shape of the figure.

70

(Incidentally it is inadvisable to attempt a photograph against the light if the sun is immediately in line with the subject and the camera. Back lighting does not mean lighting from directly behind, only that the source of light is behind the subject, the rays of the sun or other source not falling immediately on the lens.)

How, then, is it possible to introduce detail into the shadowed area? The simplest and most effective way is by using flash. It is important that the intensity of light from the flash should not balance exactly the brightness of the sun, because in that case it is quite obvious that artificial light has been used and the delicacy of the picture is sacrificed. It is all a matter of deciding how far from the subject one should stand. But the effect is good providing the distance is right and focusing accurate. Almost all modern cameras, even quite inexpensive ones, are equipped with the necessary shoe for a flash gun, and although the technique may sound rather elaborate it is really perfectly simple once it is mastered. It is one, moreover, which almost all professional photographers use, whether for portraits out of doors, or for fashion photographs, or for any subject in colour in which the contrast between highlights and shadows is great and a transparency or print without additional light on the shadowed areas is unlikely to be satisfactory.

Many cannot be bothered to have flash equipment ready for holiday snapshots. That is quite understandable, but there are other ways in which approximately the same result can be obtained. All one needs is a reflector which will reflect the light cast by the sun on to the subject of the photograph. Many kinds of reflector are manufactured and are on sale in most photographic shops. But a sheet of white paper will perform the same service almost as well as a formal reflector. Even light-coloured sand or other light foreground will reflect a good deal of light

71

back on to the subject. Clearly if this natural "reflector" is strong enough it is much to be preferred to an artificial one, because it is less likely to destroy the spontaneity of the picture.

It is an interesting, and to the amateur photographer very important, fact that skin tones often reproduce better in reflected light than in direct sunlight. If one is photographing people on a really dull day in conditions in which a blue cast is most apparent, it is worth experimenting with two U.V. filters instead of one, although it must be remembered that a slight blue cast helps to catch the spirit of a dull or rainy day when the colours as recorded by the eye are predominantly cool.

That brings us to the most important of all the factors which make for good photographs of people—the choice of background. This should always be simple. Simplicity is almost essential for the success of a picture of a single person or of a group, if only because a complex background detracts from the focus of interest. Even so, a three-dimensional effect is just as important in photographing people as in photographing any other subject, and that involves three planes, a foreground, a middle ground, and a background. Probably the best of all backgrounds in these cases is the sky, provided that the sky is not so dramatic as to dominate the rest. If one can catch a pretty girl sitting on a wall and photograph from a rather low viewpoint so that the whole figure is outlined against a pale blue sky, or for that matter against a uniformly cloudy sky, the result is almost certain to be good providing there is some minor object in the foreground to give depth to the picture. The result may be a snapshot in the ordinarily accepted sense of the term, but it may equally well be a superb photograph. Without some object in the foreground the picture may look like a posed portrait and that is something to be avoided at all costs.

The foreground object, however, need not be complex or difficult to find—some driftwood on the beach, or merely a pattern of pebbles and sand, will serve admirably.

The most important point of all in selecting a background (and backgrounds can be selected merely by changing the angle from which the photograph is being taken) is to avoid extraneous objects, such as trees or chimney stacks, which all too often seem to be springing from the head of the person photographed. That is a case where the eye of the camera is not so discriminating as the human eye. The human eye is able to neglect such extraneous objects and concentrate on the person or people being photographed. The camera eye takes equal account of everything it sees. This may sound rather self-evident, but anyone who has processed large numbers of pictures taken by beginners or by careless amateurs will agree that it is the most important of all advice, even neglected by many people whom one would expect to know better. What one has got to do is to visualise the scene in terms of the camera's eye and not in terms of the human eye.

To sum up, the first essential in photographing people is to ensure that the subjects are relaxed, preferably doing things and unaware that a picture is being taken. If that is impossible we must fall back on the second rule, which is to avoid posing the subject, because posed pictures always look posed and however skilful never give the impression of spontaneity which is the hallmark of a good picture of people. This is particularly important when photographing children, who are unduly camera conscious. It is the natural expression and reaction of a child that we want to capture rather than a formal likeness, which will always look wooden and featureless. The third rule is that brightly coloured clothes are a great help in rendering people in colour; the fourth that the background must always be subordinate to the subject being photographed. An addendum to these four rules is that if one is using a simple camera with a fixed focus one should choose a viewpoint at least ten feet away from the subject. That is not a bad rule, either, for users of more complex cameras which are capable of being focused down to three feet or less, unless one is attempting serious portraiture and using a model who is capable of looking relaxed and unself-conscious in a posed photograph.

CHAPTER 5

Photographing Buildings

Photographing buildings, villages, or scenes in towns, is, like photographing people, a specialised phase of photography and especially difficult with the standard 35 mm. camera. Ideally one needs a camera fitted with a rising front to reproduce buildings in town or country, but no 35 mm. camera is so fitted. Indeed, any camera with a rising front is hard to find, although thirty years ago a number of models were on sale and all Press cameras of to-day incorporate this feature. The real difficulty is to get far enough from a building to picture it adequately without leaving a large expanse of featureless foreground.

The difficulty can be overcome in several ways. The most obvious one is to interpolate a figure between the camera and the building. Since buildings are generally rather monochrome this figure should be as colourful as possible. It may be a girl in a red coat walking along the pavement. It may be one of one's friends deliberately interpolated into the picture to give it depth and colour. It may be a car or group of cars parked near the building. It may be a flowering tree or shrub. Whatever it is, some colourful feature is essential if the building is to be rendered adequately in a transparency or colour print.

On the other hand, the foreground object, whether a person or people, or an inanimate object, must not be dominant or it will detract from the importance of the building. Builders of the late Georgian and Regency periods were the true friends of colour photographers, because so many of the graceful frontages which they raised for instance, at Cheltenham, Brighton and Bath, were built round a square planted with trees and flowers. Some of the most attractive of all photographs of buildings are these Georgian or Regency squares, especially in springtime when the flowers are in bloom, and the trees are in bud, but are not dominant enough to obscure the beauty of the buildings behind them.

Whatever the solution determined by the layout of the buildings and their surroundings, the one thing that has to be overcome if tall buildings are to be photographed is this difficulty of dealing with the foreground. This should be in the mind of every photographer who attempts to perpetuate the beauty of an urban or a village scene.

Other devices are recommended by some photographers. One is to adopt a deliberately unnatural viewpoint looking up towards the top of the building. This causes the verticals to converge. Though in a few cases, as when photographing the tower and spire of a church, it may produce pleasing results when the tower and spire are outlined against a blue sky with white cloud, it is rarely successful with other buildings. However carefully the photograph is taken, the impression is given that the photographer has " muffed his shot."

Another device used by many professional photographers is the angle shot. This can be remarkably effective if it is quite impossible to include the whole building in a single frame, but it is a device which needs very careful use and one which with an inexperienced photographer can lead to ludicrous distortion. The basic idea behind the angle shot is that the photographer is composing a pattern, including various features of the building without regard to its shape or its position in relation to other buildings. It can be uncommonly successful when it is a matter of photographing a frieze or pediment on a classical building, sometimes also when photographing the clerestory or other elevated parts of a church.

The angle chosen is usually diagonally across the frame from bottom left to top right. It makes little difference, however, what angle is selected so long as the resulting picture has a pleasing design and sufficient detail and colour to make it an attractive transparency or colour print.

Blue sky as a background is a tremendous help. Alternatively a dark or thundery sky as the background of a building which is predominantly white or light-coloured can be most effective. Contrast is essential and the lines of the building must be shown in bold relief against the background. At the same time, the background itself must never be a dominant feature of the photograph, as it might well be if the sky is a very dramatic one and the building relatively featureless. It is all a matter of arrangement, and arrangement is far more within the scope of the photographer of buildings than it is within that of the photographer of landscapes or of people. The aim, as always, is to take a picture which pleases, rather than one which has technical excellence or conforms to the rules of composition.

Unfortunately nature does not always arrange the surroundings of a building or group of buildings in a way which is helpful to the photographer. Getting rid of unwanted features is just as important as inserting a suitable foreground when photographing buildings. The very trees which in early spring can make such an effective frame or foreground for a group of Regency buildings can obscure them completely in summer. No sound advice can be given on how to obviate this difficulty except that the quality of the picture depends almost entirely on the viewpoint from which it is taken. If there is no suitable viewpoint, then the picture should not be taken. But it is amazing how often a good viewpoint can be found with patience, always having regard to the colour values of the foreground, the building itself, and the background, which is normally sky. Assuming that a particular building is the central motif, the building should not be in the centre of the frame, nor should it be at either edge. Ideally it should be slightly to the left or right of the centre and it is most important to find the best viewpoint to ensure that the top of the building is not cut off and that there is enough sky visible to provide a contrasting colour.

All that has been said so far applies to the photography of whole buildings, but many excellent photographs can be taken of details, of doors, or windows, or even—if the focusing device attached to the camera will allow focusing down to three feet or less—of still more apparently insignificant parts of a building such as a door-knocker or a carved ornament. In such cases neither foreground nor background offers any difficulty because the whole picture is occupied by the detail being photographed, but obviously colour is of the utmost importance. Many subjects of this kind which are admirably reproduced in monochrome photography are quite useless for colour. During the last ten years, however, there has been a growing tendency to introduce colour into the frontages of houses and public buildings. A red-painted door, a blue or yellow-painted window with window boxes containing gaily-coloured flowers—these are ideal subjects so long as there is a contrast between the colours.

Design is most important, just as it is in monochrome, but the photographer in colour has a wonderful opportunity to render detail in its natural colours and produce pictures which are not only faithful renderings of the subject but also have real aesthetic value. Great care must be taken to avoid over-exposure, for over-exposure blots out the highlights and dims the bright colours which appeal to the eye. It is better to give an aperture of half a stop less than that recommended by the manufacturers of the film, especially if the photograph is designed for a transparency to be projected on a ground-glass screen. In photographing buildings, slight under-exposure is always to be preferred to over-exposure. Under-exposure, although it may prevent any detail appearing in the shadowed areas, brings out the bright colours of the buildings in their natural hues.

In this connection, buildings with red roofs, so common in the countryside, or red brick farmhouses, are ideal subjects, especially when there is a green foreground suitably broken up and a background composed of sky, with at least some blue patches against which the red roof or red bricks stand out with startling clarity.

When photographing people or landscapes one can usually select the angle of lighting. That is not possible when picturing buildings except to a limited degree. Yet lighting is vital in the production of a good print or transparency. The conventional advice to beginners is to use front lighting only, that is to say, to take photographs only when the sun is shining directly on the subject. That is most misleading. Few buildings have enough prominent features to make a good picture with frontal lighting, which destroys the impression of depth. Side lighting, or rather lighting when the sun is at an angle of about 45 degrees to the building, is far better. Then the shadows cast by eaves, window frames, or door frames emphasise the features of the building and provided they are not too long it does not matter if no detail is shown within the shadowed area.

This use of shadows is well known to most photographers in black and white but it is not used nearly as frequently by photographers in the new medium of colour. It depends on the film used how effective these shadows can be. Shadows cast by very slow reversal film such as Kodachrome I are particularly effective. The rendering of shadows by the fast films is less effective but still serves to give the impression of depth and shape to a building. Briefly, what one has to avoid is taking a photograph which reveals only a flat face, featureless and unrelieved, while the greater the variety of colour that can be introduced, the better the picture is likely to be.

Again, when photographing buildings it is unnecessary to follow the advice of most film manufacturers to confine photography to the period between two or three hours after sunrise and two or three hours before sunset. Admittedly outside these limits the rendering of the colour of the building will be rather warmer than it appears in nature, but that is not always a disadvantage. Moreover, it will be necessary either to double the exposure, or to open the lens by between half a stop and a full stop more than at midday, especially in the evening when there is usually more haze in the atmosphere than in the morning. An exposure meter even of the most efficient kind will not always solve the problem, because the reading it gives if it is pointed towards a building will often be almost identical for a sunlit subject an hour before sunset and near midday. Experience is the best guide but the simple rule of increasing the exposure or the aperture quite automatically during the hour or two before sunset is an adequate guide in normal circumstances.

Incidentally, some very fine shots in colour can be obtained when the sunlight is almost parallel with the face of a building, that is, when the shadows are long and quite a large part of the face of the building is obscured by them. Such a photograph, however, will not be a record picture but rather an essay in pictorial photography. Its success will depend entirely on the inspiration of the photographer, the exposure given, and the angle chosen.

Although, as we have already seen, back lighting can be effective for action shots of people, it cannot be recom-

The blue of sea and the sky, the impression of lazy holidays in the sun, the colourful character of the Mediterranean—all these are captured in this photograph of a beach on Capri. *Kodak Ektachrome film. Photo by A. K. Phillip.*

This photograph of the Chess Valley shows the value of figures in the foreground to give perspective to a landscape. It also illustrates the eye-catching value of a splash of red. *Kodak Ektachrome film.*

mended for buildings, although it is well worth an experiment or two to see what results can be achieved. Occasionally with a white or cream building which has some contrast the result may be satisfactory, but the exposure given must be that for shadow, not for highlights, otherwise the whole point of the photograph will be lost and the transparency or negative grossly under-exposed. It follows that when attempting shots such as these it is better to exclude the sky, which is an unwanted highlight and will show little or no colour because of the length of the exposure. Sunlit highlights in the foreground also should be excluded because the colours of these will be washed out for the same reason. Except in rare instances the technique of photographing buildings against the light is only practicable when the building itself has exceptional colour contrasts and its features are sufficiently well marked to make a pattern.

The shape of the picture of a building is important. It may seem obvious that a landscape shape picture gives an impression of width, an upright picture an impression of height, but it is a truth which seems to be lost on many photographers, experienced ones as well as beginners. What the photographer has to do is to decide whether the general impression of the building is one of breadth or of height. If the former, a means must be found to photograph it horizontally, if the latter, vertically.

Some authorities take the view that all transparencies should be horizontal so that when they are projected they give an impression of uniformity. In theory that may be good advice but in practice it limits the scope of photographing buildings to a rather absurd degree, if only because there are so many buildings which cannot possibly be pictured satisfactorily in a horizontal frame. Many Victorian, Georgian, and 20th-century buildings or groups of buildings depend for their very character on their height.

81

To take an extreme example, it is scarcely conceivable that the skyscrapers of New York could be pictured adequately on a landscape shape photograph. What, then, of the post-war office blocks of the City of London, of the new and colourful buildings in Dover, or of the Civic Centre of Southampton, of which the essential character is that it towers towards the sky and seems to be reaching out an arm to link the earth with the heavens. Surely such pictures and thousands of others demand an upright frame if their character is to be reproduced. If the interpolation of an upright frame during the projection of a number of slides produces a discordant note, it will also jar the audience into paying special attention to that particular picture. There are far too many conventions in photography and this is one which is best neglected.

If one is using a square frame, as with the 12 on 120 type of camera, the problem does not arise. Both the normal $2\frac{1}{4}'' \times 2\frac{1}{4}''$ transparency and the slightly smaller " super slide " are suited to picturing buildings because both width and height can be suggested by altering the viewpoint. For this kind of picture the square format is a better all-purpose size than the miniature 35 mm. one. The prejudice against square pictures is gradually disappearing as more and more people use this format, but it must be admitted that many inexperienced observers still feel that an oblong is to be preferred to a square, while many photographers in black and white who use a square format, as on Rolleiflex cameras, do so only with the idea of trimming the prints to an oblong shape. That unfortunately is not possible with transparencies except by masking them.

So far we have been thinking principally of picturing an individual building of special interest or a group of buildings of homogeneous character. Many of the finest colour photographs, however, are of whole villages or of characteristic scenes in towns. The difficulties of photographing the latter are precisely the same as those of photographing individual buildings. But colour photography of villages presents some rather special problems, though they are relatively easy to overcome.

The greatest problem is to avoid major contrasts between areas of well-lighted buildings and areas of shade. In this the problem of the photographer in colour is very similar to that of the photographer in black and white. It is impossible to expose correctly both for highlights and for shadowed areas. Either the shadow areas will be without detail or else the highlights will be burnt out. The shadowed areas in sunny weather must be small and must lead the eye to some major feature in the photograph. Otherwise they will spoil the picture. In cloudy conditions, providing the camera used is sufficiently adaptable, the problem is far easier, so long as there is enough colour in the buildings of the village to make an attractive picture without the help of the sun.

Difficult though it may seem to secure the right lighting and the right subject, village photography is wonderfully rewarding. A stream or pond makes a perfect foreground, as in the innumerable pictures which have been taken of Finchingfield in Essex, in which the composition of the picture is dependent on the foreground blue of the water, the mixture of red brick and colour-washed houses building up to the tower of the church sharply etched against a blue and white sky. The stream which runs through Castle Combe in Wiltshire provides an equally satisfactory foreground, with the mellow stone bridge and the cottages rising towards the ancient market cross.

Any reader can think of similar examples in his own part of the country. All that is needed is colour contrast, preferably one which consists of a cool colour like blue and a warm colour such as that of Cotswold stone or red brick. We must beware, however, of making too much use of colourful cottage gardens in composing a colour photograph. Many village gardens are an absolute riot of colour, promising an exciting transparency or colour print, but the results are nearly always disappointing. The colours when transferred to a print or transparency give only a patchwork effect with which the eye cannot cope, while the cottage or house for which the flower garden seemed in nature to be such an effective foreground is entirely dominated by it. When the colours are massed in a garden, as happens all too seldom, then the garden is a perfect foreground providing its colours are not dominant enough to destroy the colour values of the house. That does not mean that flower gardens are unsuitable subjects for colour. Often they make beautiful photographs. But it is necessary to make up one's mind whether one is photographing a garden or a house. The average country garden in its summer splendour is an unsuitable foreground if the house behind it is intended to be the central feature of the photograph.

The buildings of the countryside, farmhouses or village homes, present hundreds of suitable subjects but it is necessary to be discriminating. It is possible to go many miles along roads or footpaths without finding anything which really calls for rendering in colour and then come across a village or a group of homesteads which have infinite possibilities. Churches, inns with their colourful signs, windmills (remembering that white is an excellent foil for other colours), bridges, manor-houses, thatched cottages—all these are the ingredients of admirable colour photographs and are generally much easier to include in the composition of a good photograph than town houses or town scenes. But it is futile to waste film on subjects which do not possess the necessary contrasts in colour or the harmony of line to make a pleasing composition.

CHAPTER 6

Photographing Landscapes

It is always unsatisfactory to give negative advice rather than positive, to start with don'ts rather than dos. But that seems the only way to introduce the subject of landscape photography in colour, which is not by any means as easy as it looks and, as most amateurs and professionals alike would agree, is more difficult than photographing groups of people in suitable conditions or than photographing villages or colourful buildings.

Two major faults spoil a great number of the colour prints and transparencies produced by beginners. The first and the most lethal is the inclusion of an expanse of unrelieved green in the foreground. The second, almost as frequent but not quite so fatal to the quality of the photograph, is the bluish tinge which spoils the effect of many distant landscapes. Both these faults can be avoided, and must be, if the colour prints or transparencies are to be fair representations of the scenes depicted.

It must be remembered that the dominant colour of most lowland landscapes is green. The photographer has to make a careful choice of viewpoint and of subject matter in order to avoid a picture which looks merely an essay in green. However restful that colour may be to the eye, it needs enlivening with other colours to make a good picture.

Colour film is rather more kind to unrelieved foregrounds than monochrome, because it brings out more clearly the differences in tone between one shade of green and another, but the differences in tones are not sufficient to make a pleasing picture. It is a wonderful feeling when we have reached the summit of some hill and look down on an expanse of green fields picked out by clumps of trees and hedges. What a wonderful view, we say, and point our camera at it, make a suitable exposure, and then await the inevitable disappointment when the film has been processed of seeing a picture which lacks depth, colour, and variety, the three essential ingredients of a good landscape photograph.

The moorlands and mountains are not much easier to photograph, except when the heather is in bloom. The permanent colour of the moorlands is grey and this is not well conveyed by colour film unless relieved and given point by other colours, while many hills are as green as the lowlands. Even mountains are generally devoid of colour in themselves, or rather of variety in colouring, with a few significant exceptions, such as the snow-capped mountains of Switzerland and the reddish-brown Torridon sandstone hills of Scotland. It is always necessary to remember that the eye of the camera lacks the versatility of the human eye. The human eye sees what it wants to see and has the ability to leap over dull foregrounds and concentrate on the middle distance or on the background. The camera eye sees exactly what is in front of it and if an unrelieved expanse of one colour, whether grey or green, is in the foreground, that expanse will dominate the whole picture, however sensitive the film may be to slight differences in tone.

Avoiding this monotony of foreground or monotony of colour over the whole picture is the most important as well as the most difficult part of photographing landscapes. The other fault, the introduction of a blue cast, is easier to correct. All that is needed is the intelligent use of a U.V. filter. The exact conditions in which this filter is advisable cannot be defined. All that can be said is that it is essential for the photographing of snow-covered scenes and in general for photographing mountains and high hills. But it is also worth using one when photographing distant landscapes, and especially for cliff and downland scenes in clear weather when the blue of the sea is a dominant factor. Almost all colour films, negative and reversal, are slightly over-sensitive to blue, but this over-sensitiveness is often an advantage and only experience can show precisely when the picture is improved by fitting a U.V. filter.

It cannot be stressed too often that the choice of film is one of the most important factors in making good transparencies. All colour films, if correctly handled and given approximately the right exposure, will cope adequately with landscapes. Many fine landscape photographs are taken on Kodachrome, Ektachrome, Ilfochrome and Agfacolor, and also on their negative equivalents. But probably the best over-all results are given by Adox, which though its colours are slightly muted compared with some of the others, renders the blue of the sky, and the green of fields and trees, and the yellow of flowers with remarkable faithfulness and is less liable than several of the others to the blue cast on distant landscapes.

How, then, shall we put colour into our pictures when the prevailing colour of most landscapes is either green or grey? The simple answer, though in practice it is not quite as simple as it sounds, is to look for a splash of colour, preferably red, in a landscape and make that the focal point of the picture. Many agricultural machines, especially tractors and most combine harvesters, are painted red, and these are absolute godsends to the photographer whose chief interest is landscapes. Once one begins to look for these splashes of colour one will be surprised how often they occur and will be amazed at the difference which their inclusion in a picture makes to the print or transparency.

By the sea there are often red painted boats—fishing boats or pleasure boats—which make all the difference to a beach or harbour scene. In fact it is seldom difficult by the seashore to find a splash of colour. The art of photography is to make that splash of colour the central feature of the picture, and to choose a viewpoint which makes it the focal point of the photograph.

It is impossible always to find a tractor or combine harvester suitably positioned, but there are many other features of the countryside which can be used in the same way—a red-roofed barn or a colour-washed cottage in the middle distance, or indeed any feature which makes a contrast with the prevailing greens.

If all else fails a ploughed field will often supply the necessary contrast. There are some parts of the country in which the land is almost entirely green pasture but in the majority of districts, even in pastoral areas, there are a few ploughed fields lying fallow for most of the year. A newly ploughed field is the best of all subjects to provide the contrast in colour and although the colour of soils varies throughout Britain, most are interesting in photographic terms. The finest of all are the bright red sandstones of Devonshire and Herefordshire, but the luminous browns of the Yorkshire hills and of most of southern and eastern England are almost equally suitable.

Films which have a tendency to brighten red will bring out even more colour in these brown fields than the eye sees, and that may well be an advantage in the finished print or transparency. It is a mistake, however, to treat ploughed fields as a foreground where they will dominate the picture and prevent a balanced view of the whole scene. On the other hand, if they are too far in the background their colours may well be muted and they will be unlikely to supply the necessary contrast.

The other main problem facing the landscape photographer in colour is how to achieve an impression of depth. Some colour landscape pictures are almost stereoscopic in effect. Colour lends itself far better than black and white to achieving the three-dimensional effect which often lifts quite an ordinary scene into the sphere of really first-class photography. In monochrome photography the advice usually given is to choose some dark foreground subject, a long shadow, for instance, or a gate or a hedge. In colour work a foreground shadow is overpowering, a gate generally uninteresting, though a colourful hedge may be suitable. The principle remains the same, namely, to include three distinct planes in the picture—a foreground, a middle ground, and a background—the difference between monochrome and colour photography being that contrasting colours are the key to success in colour photography, whereas the interplay of shadowed and sunlit areas is the essence of a good landscape in monochrome.

What, then, will take the place of the long shadow or the gate, such faithful allies of the monochrome photographer? The simple answer is contained in the phrase " colourful figures " and preferably figures giving the impression of movement. All one need do to demonstrate this truth is to compare a transparency of a scene taken without figures and the same scene taken with figures in the foreground. With a group of people walking or merely sitting and looking animated in the foreground, there is an enhanced impression of depth. Providing the people are not too close to the camera they do not in any way dominate the picture of the landscape. They form part of it and give it that additional interest which the eye demands. It does not matter how the people are dressed as long as their clothes are brightly coloured, though red clothes give the most dramatic effect, blue the least dramatic. But yellows and greens and pastel shades are perfectly satisfactory. Even one figure suitably positioned will give the desired impression of depth and the bright colour in the foreground so essential to break up the greens of the rest of the landscape, and it is well worth while interpolating such a figure in the landscape if that is possible.

If it is impossible to provide people as a foreground, animals will serve the need almost as well. Horses are particularly photogenic, but a herd of Hereford or Friesian cattle, or any other colourful breed, will achieve the same purpose providing they are arranged harmoniously in the picture—and that is largely a matter of choosing the right viewpoint. One must not even despise the homely sheep. Oddly, white is excellent for colour photography, especially on films which have overcome the tendency to reproduce white as a rather dirty shade of light cream. Certainly white breaks up green extremely well but one must take one's sheep unawares because sheep have a tendency when they are aware of a human being near them to turn their backs and retreat from the foreground at considerable speed. One must remember, too, that sheep are comparatively small animals and if they are to be used to break up the green of a foreground the nearest one should be considerably nearer the camera than is desirable in the case of cattle or other relatively large animals.

Flowering trees can be used in their season with as good effect as human beings or animals. In spring the white flowers of the wild cherry and the pink of the crab apple can make a landscape photograph a picture of exceptional beauty rather than an ordinary record photograph of a well known scene.

In autumn the colour photographer comes into his own

when the leaves of the trees, especially of beech trees, turn from green to russet brown and gold and red and dominate the greens of the rest of the landscape. There is no need to be afraid of over-emphasising these autumn tints, which are the colours of nature and wonderfully recorded by most reversal films. A single tree can be photographed to good effect, or a whole wood in which the colours vary from green to red, or a coppice or strip of woodland can be used to give point to a wider landscape.

Holly is a help too, with its strong contrast between the red berries and the green leaves, giving colour to many winter landscapes which otherwise would not deserve the exposure of a colour film. Unhappily, holly is a very variable factor. In some winters there are scarcely any berries, in others the red is too insistent for a good photograph. However, whether it is a good year or a poor one, holly bushes are worth looking for, especially in evergreen countryside such as that of the sandstone hills of Surrey, where on a bright day, even in December or January, fascinating studies can be taken of the pine trees and dead bracken enlivened by the lighter greens and reds of the holly bushes.

The same is true of many of the woodland areas of Sussex and of other parts of the country where pine trees flourish and there are also holly bushes, making it possible to picture colourful scenes at a time of year when some of the brightest colours have disappeared from the countryside and when most people would think that only monochrome could reproduce the beauty of the scene.

A favourite way of giving the impression of depth to landscape photographs is to include a stream, preferably one which enters the picture at the bottom left and flows towards the top right. This is the equivalent in colour photography of the track or road which leads the eye in monochrome pictures from left through the centre to the top right. A clear stream, preferably one with boulders (relieving the blue of the stream) is the best of all friends of the colour photographer and is the making of many pictures in hill country and mountains, even when the rest of the scene is a uniform grey or grey-green. If a stone bridge spans the stream, so much the better, because that gives an additional colour and adds variety. The ideal is a stream which leads the eye conclusively towards a strong background, reflecting the blue of a sky which is itself enlivened with white cumulus clouds. Then one has blues and greens and whites in the picture and with a little luck some intermediate tones as well.

Yellow flowers are a help in such a situation and as yellow flowers are particularly common in some kinds of mountain country, it follows that many fine pictures can be composed with their help. The moorlands, for instance, which fall away from the Arenigs in Central Wales may seem at first sight to be featureless, yet by the banks of the numerous streams which flow through them there are many clumps of flowers. Similarly in the Peak District of Derbyshire many of the tiny streams flowing into the Dove are lined with yellow musk, which makes the scene especially attractive as rendered by a transparency or colour print.

The variations on this theme are limitless. All that is needed is to find a place where there is a real contrast between colours—between the green or grey of the fields or moors, the blue of a stream, and the colour of the flowers or plants near its banks—to ensure an outstanding colour picture. If there should be a figure in the foreground, so much the better, but it is not essential.

In Scotland, Switzerland, Norway, and many other countries, lakes or inlets of the sea will take the place of streams, providing that they do not fill the greater part of the photograph. The inland lochs of Scotland are particularly effective as foregrounds, especially if the photographer chooses a high angle from which he can see the whole width of the loch with some green or brown or red in the foreground and mountains in the background, preferably snow-covered, but at least contrasting strongly with the blue of the loch and the green of the reeds or grass.

The same technique can be employed with ponds and lakes in the lowlands, sometimes even more effectively, because there is often more choice of foreground. Waggoners Wells near Hindhead in Surrey can provide a magnificent colour picture in autumn, when the leaves of the trees are turning brown and the sky is still blue enough to colour the water of the ponds, where the causeways between one pond and another stand out clearly with their dun colouring, and the golden brown of the leaves is reflected in the water. At Waggoners Wells, as in so many other artificial sheets of water, there are swans which, with their graceful shapes and white plumage, add immeasurably to the beauty of the picture.

One might go on indefinitely. One can make a picture for oneself, one does not have to wait for nature to make one. One can see the valley of the Seph in Yorkshire with reddish brown cows in the foreground, green trees in the middle plane, and ploughed fields in the background. One can see Bamburgh Castle on the coast of Northumberland, with almost white sand and green-covered dunes in the foreground, and the mellow hues of the castle rising above the blue of the sea in the middle distance. One can see any lake in Cumberland or Westmorland with the blue water broken by boats or by rocks and the dark screes of the mountains rising beyond. There is no lack of subjects, but every subject (and every viewpoint) has to be chosen carefully if the results are to be attractive and if the photographer is to feel that he has captured the spirit of nature and the essential quality of the countryside.

Some professional photographers claim that no landscape photograph is successful unless it has a bright splash of colour in the foreground. That is a sweeping statement and like all sweeping statements omits part of the truth. There must certainly be a bright splash of colour somewhere in the photograph if it is to make a lasting impression, but this colourful area need not be in the foreground. However, it is true that many pictures are made particularly attractive by a mass of colour in the foreground. A Cornish fishing village may provide rather a dull picture in colour by itself but if it is photographed with a foreground of hydrangeas, the most characteristic of all Cornish flowers, it will take on a completely new character and stand out in memory when many other pictures have been forgotten. Flowering trees or plants always make a good foreground if the camera one is using is capable of giving sufficient depth of field to bring the foreground objects into sharp focus and also the scenic background. With simple cameras landscapes are better photographed at infinity with no prominent subject closer than 10 ft. Similarly, in dull weather, even when one is using a more versatile camera, foreground subjects can give great difficulty with the comparatively slow films which are generally used.

Framing a picture is commonplace for photographers in black and white. Something has already been said of this matter in relation to composition but the principles of framing in monochrome and colour are quite different. One of the most useful frames for a colour picture is two trees in full foliage. But it is essential that the objects which make the frame, whether trees or any other feature of the countryside, should not be dominant in colour. Blues and greens are good for framing but not reds, because red is a dominant colour and the frame will tend to override the colour values of the rest of the picture. In spite of the pitfalls of framing in colour, the idea is a good one and should be followed when possible, provided that the colours are suitable and the subject lends itself to this treatment.

That only leaves us with one problem but a very difficult as well as a very important one, that of keeping the horizon horizontal. A horizontal horizon is just as important in landscape photographs as verticals are in photographs of buildings, yet how few people realise this, or give the necessary attention to it when composing their pictures. It is all the more important when reversal film is used since control during processing is impossible. A transparency cannot be " trimmed." Yet of every hundred landscape pictures taken by amateurs, not necessarily beginners at that, nearly half show a horizon which is not strictly horizontal, and that spoils the picture.

Yet correction of this fault is only a matter of attention and concentration. Whatever the camera that is being used, the view-finder is the guide. With a reflex camera, whether single or twin lens, there is no excuse for making a mistake, and very little more with a camera equipped with an eye-level view-finder. Most people are so keen on composing their picture that they do not notice the line of the horizon and are disappointed when the finished print or transparency shows a horizon out of true.

CHAPTER 7

Photographing in Colour Indoors

Many think of colour photography as a hobby only for summer holidays or summer weekends. Many more think of it as a hobby only for out of doors whether in summer or winter. Neither of those views represents the truth. Colour film can be used for photography indoors just as well as out of doors and it provides a wonderful hobby for the dark months of winter, when outdoor work is difficult. All that is needed is a reasonably versatile camera—a camera which has at least a variable focus and aperture. Add to that a range-finder, even of the most simple kind, and if possible an exposure meter, and you have everything that is needed to take exciting and interesting pictures of anything from a baby in the bath to a Christmas party—apart, that is, from providing the light necessary to take pictures.

There are four ways of providing this light. The first is to use available light, that is, to take pictures by the light filtering through the windows of a room in daylight. The second way is by the use of photoflood lights with or without the help of normal electric lighting. The third, and the most popular method, is by the use of a flash gun and expendable flash bulbs. The fourth is with the help of an electronic flash gun, which produces results very similar to those achieved with the use of expendable flash bulbs but is more economical if many pictures are going to be taken in a relatively short space of time, but far more expensive in view of the high cost of the equipment if only a few are likely to be taken. Each of these four methods

There is no need to put the camera away when winter approaches. Freshly fallen snow transforms the character of the best-known scenes, as here in London's Regent's Park. *Kodak Kodachrome II film. Photo by Christopher Trent.*

After winter, spring, when the first flowers bring colour to the monochrome winter scene, like these celandines photographed near Crawley, Hampshire. *Perutz film. Photo by Christopher Trent.*

Colourful flower beds add to the beauty of many photographs of houses and cottages, but it is important that the flower beds should not be a jumble of colours and should have a dominant colour theme, as here in the garden of a house at Higher Denham. *Kodak Ektachrome film.*

has advantages and disadvantages but all four are highly practical and do not involve any great knowledge or experience on the part of the photographer.

Colour photography indoors is different in many ways from monochrome. One reason is that colour films generally are rather slower than monochrome ones and apart from H.S. Ektachrome no colour film, either reversal or negative, approaches the speed of the high-speed monochrome films. This fact obviously means a larger aperture or a longer exposure, or both, thus reducing the depth of field, that is, the area in sharp focus. Again, it is apparent that many photographs taken indoors are spoilt by the combination of over-exposure of the highlights in the foreground and under-exposure of the background, draining the picture of bright colours and making it much less satisfactory than a similar shot taken with black and white film. However, a little care will prevent this, while it is true to say that many indoor photographs taken by relatively inexperienced amateurs with simple equipment make excellent transparencies for projection, or negatives from which pleasing paper prints can be made.

A vital difference between photographing in colour in daylight and in artificial light is that the qualities of the two lights are different. Normal artificial light has a yellowish tinge which spoils the effect of film designed primarily for outdoor photography but this difference can be overcome by the use of appropriate filters, while several manufacturers produce films specially designed for artificial light. Light which approximates to daylight can be produced by the use of blue flash bulbs or electronic flash so that daylight film can be used.

The whole subject of indoor photography is overlaid with technical terms which are quite unnecessary and which serve only to bewilder the beginner into thinking that the subject is far more technical than it really is. Tungsten lighting, for instance, which is frequently quoted in books on photography and in the brochures issued by film and bulb manufacturers, means no more than ordinary artificial lighting produced by an electric bulb. Once this point has been grasped the whole matter becomes far more simple and the problems, if there are any, of photographing in artificial light become capable of easy solution.

It must have become apparent to every reader of this book by now that negative films are not so popular as reversal films except in the most simple of cameras which do not have a lens with variable aperture. However, it must be admitted that because negative films have a greater latitude than reversal films they are in some ways particularly suited to photographing indoors in circumstances in which estimation of the light values is far more difficult than it would be out of doors. Providing that the exposure and aperture have been determined correctly, with or without the help of an exposure meter, colour negative films can be used indoors with ordinary artificial lighting (including photoflood) without a filter, in exactly the same way as monochrome films. If flash bulbs are used they should be white.

It has been said earlier that the exposure latitude of negative colour films is in the range of two stops. It follows that the variety of detail which can be obtained in artificial light is very much greater than if a reversal film is used. Even so, the colour rendering is not usually as good as that of a reversal film and the increased area in which detail can be recorded is as often an embarrassment as an advantage, because it tends to detract from the importance of the main subject of interest.

Any type of reversal film designed for use in daylight can be used for indoor photography with a flash gun and blue flash bulbs. If tungsten lighting only is available a conversion filter must be used. It is probably better, however, to use one of the films which are manufactured especially for indoor photography. These include Koda-chrome Type A, Ektachrome Type F, Ferraniacolor Type A, and Ilford Colour Type F. These are all rather slow but are perfectly adequate for the purpose which they are meant to serve and quite easy to use, though a tripod is a great advantage. The speed of Kodachrome I Type A is 16 A.S.A., equivalent to 23° B.S. Ilford Colour and Ektachrome Type F are almost identical in speed. Ferraniacolor Type A is faster, with an A.S.A. rating of 25, B.S. 25° and Kodachrome II Type A is rated 40 A.S.A., 27° B.S. Agfacolor C.K.20 is a recent addition to the range of films. It is faster than the others listed with an A.S.A. rating of 80, i.e. 30° B.S. Its emulsion is adapted only to the colour temperature of normal photo-flood lighting. All these films are available in standard cassettes for miniature 35 mm. cameras. The Ektachrome Type F is also produced for 120/620 roll film cameras and the Ferraniacolor Type A for 127 size roll film cameras, as well as for 120/620.

When these films specially designed for tungsten light-ing are exposed it is essential that a tungsten light should be used, i.e. clear flash bulbs, never blue ones, photo-floods or normal artificial illumination. It is worth remembering that conversion filters are available for these tungsten light films to make them suitable for use in daylight, but the use of conversion filters is not recom-mended and it is far better to use film designed for arti-ficial light in artificial light only. The converse is not so true. The conversion filters available for making daylight films suitable for artificial lighting are remarkably effective, and if the object is merely to take two or three photo-graphs on a special occasion the purchase of a conversion filter, which need cost only a few shillings, is well worth while.

The manufacturers say that Ektachrome, whether normal or high speed, can be used with photoflood or other normal artificial lighting if a U.V. filter is fitted. One of the specially designed conversion filters is better. Different conversion filters are recommended by different film manufacturers and it is always worth while to discover from a photographic dealer the filter which is most suitable for the film being used. However, there is no real difficulty about obtaining the necessary information and no major expense entailed. The most important rule to bear in mind is that blue flash bulbs and electronic flash give light very similar to that of natural daylight, so that daylight films can be used without a filter while all other sources of artificial lighting distort the colour rendering of the film and must be used with an appropriate filter, which is designed to make light falling on the lens similar to that of daylight. The wise thing to do is to follow the instructions contained in the leaflet which is packed with every roll of colour film, whatever its country of origin, although it must be admitted that some of the instructions issued need very careful reading before they are intelligible.

That is especially true of some of the excellent German films, such as Perutz. In each roll of Perutz film the following instruction appears: " Artificial light. C 18 daylight film can be used with different types of artificial lighting. If approximation of artificial light to characteristics of daylight is required, a correction filter must be used according to the indication of a colour temperature meter. For photofloods, for example, a blue B 12 filter (filter factor $1\frac{1}{2}$ stops) and for usual electric bulbs a B 18 filter (filter factor $2\frac{1}{2}$ stops) is recommended. Mixing daylight and artificial light results in colour variations."

Once the precise meaning of this has been mastered (and it is only a matter of careful reading) all the knowledge necessary for using this and similar films in artificial lighting conditions has been obtained. Similar instructions are issued with most other films which are described as universal, by which is meant that although they are designed primarily for use in daylight they can also be used in artificial light.

Many amateurs avoid colour photographs indoors because they fear that the price will be prohibitive. If they have a suitable camera, however, the price is remarkably low if one remembers the pleasure and satisfaction which indoor colour pictures can give. The cost of the film and processing is identical with that of photographs taken outdoors. The means of supplying sufficient artificial light adds to the cost but here again the additional cost is not nearly as great as many people believe. All cameras except the most simple ones have built-in shoes for flash guns. The cost of a reliable flash gun is as low as 30/- and a really excellent one can be purchased for a few pounds. Expendable flash bulbs, that is, flash bulbs which can only be used for one photograph, are less than 1/- each—at the time of writing 8d.—the blue flash bulbs being slightly more expensive than the white ones. This means that, using flash, transparencies can be obtained for well under 2/- each.

If electronic flash is used, the initial expenditure is much greater, the cost of an electronic flash gun of a reliable make being little under £20, but a great number of exposures can be made before the apparatus wears out. Indeed, the initial cost, even if it is as high as £20, is quickly recovered if the number of pictures being taken is large.

Photoflood lighting is also relatively inexpensive providing that the lamps are switched on only for the time necessary to take the picture and not, as so many beginners believe, for the duration of a party or any other event at which indoor photographs are to be taken. But if photofloods are used it is almost essential to have two or more lamps so as to fill in the ugly and distracting shadows which result if a single photoflood lamp is used.

The greatest difficulty in taking pleasing pictures in colour indoors is the choice of subject. People are obviously good subjects, so are arrangements of brightly coloured flowers, preferably in vases of pastel shades. There are hundreds of other subjects almost equally suitable but the essential quality of each is that it should present a definite focus of colour interest in one plane, while exact focusing on this plane is of paramount importance. The reason is that whatever type of artificial lighting is used, the intensity of the light falls off very sharply beyond a certain point. Unless a number of photoflood lamps are used it is almost impossible to photograph a whole room, because, however carefully and accurately the aperture and exposure are chosen, if the foreground is correctly exposed the background must inevitably be grossly under-exposed.

This is virtually the only limiting factor, but it is one to be borne in mind even if the photographs are being taken indoors by daylight. Either the whole subject must be in the sunlight coming through a window or it must be wholly in a well lighted area but out of the range of the rays of the sun. Also the intensity of daylight falls off sharply the farther the subject is from the window. These variations in light do not matter as much in the case of monochrome because of the greater latitude of the film. However, it is only a matter of applying the lessons learned out of doors to a different medium. In the same way it is important that no reflecting surface, such as the glass front of a bookcase, should be within the direct line of the camera's vision. If it is, flare will result and the colours of the picture will be spoilt. Even a highly polished door can spoil the effect and it is a good rule to make certain that whatever background is directly facing the camera has a completely matt surface.

Another point of significance is that the subject being photographed must be placed in such a way that it stands out from its background. This again is a matter of applying the lessons learned out of doors but is more important in indoor photography. To name an outstanding example, the photograph of a person, however accurately taken, however pleasing its colours, will not give a good effect if the subject is not several feet from a wall. The tones of the wall, which are likely to be under-exposed if the subject is correctly exposed, will provide only a dark and troublesome background, detracting from the natural colours of the main subject.

It has been said that posed pictures are rarely pleasing. That is equally true in theory of pictures taken indoors as of those taken in the open air, but it is a great deal more difficult to take unposed pictures indoors in view of the exact focusing necessary and the comparative lack of penetration of artificial light as compared with sunlight. For the beginner, therefore, it is probably better to forget the rule and start by taking rather carefully posed pictures indoors until confidence has been obtained and the limitations of colour photography indoors have been proved by experience.

Happily there are many still-life subjects, such as flowers, which do not show the self-consciousness of human models and these are recommended for the complete beginner. When arranging them all that is necessary is to remember, firstly, that they should be in a single plane, and, secondly, that the most pleasing pictures will result if they present contrasting masses of colour, while conversely if they are fussy in arrangement with many slightly varying splashes of colour the result is bound to be unsatisfactory. This is only a variation on the advice given earlier on photographing gardens and landscapes.

A large number of flash guns are on the market. All, or almost all, of them are satisfactory in use within their capacity but, as with all other photographic equipment, it is wise to buy the most expensive that one can afford. To quote just one example, two Adox flash guns are marketed, the Electra I and the Electra II. The Electra I is a stream-lined light-weight flash gun, with a bulb ejector and an exposure calculator on the back of the casing. It costs about thirty shillings. The Electra II is an equally light and similarly backed flash gun with a collapsible reflector, a bulb ejector knob, and a flexibly mounted condenser held in position by two clips. It costs approximately £1 more than the Electra I but the difference in usefulness is well worth the higher price.

Almost every manufacturer produces flash guns of similar performance. However bewildering it may seem to the beginner to choose from so many, the likelihood is that the one chosen will prove perfectly satisfactory in use. A collapsible reflector is obviously a great help for two reasons, first, that a reflector intensifies the light available and helps it to penetrate, and second, that a collapsible type makes transport easy.

When flash bulbs are being used, an exposure of ap-proximately 1/30th of a second is recommended. This relatively long exposure is necessary to ensure that the whole of the "flash" (approximately 1/50th of a second) is used. When photoflood lights are used the exposure can only be determined with the help of an exposure meter. When electronic flash is employed the exposure can be as brief as desired, certainly not more than 1/100th of a second, the actual duration of the flash being 1/300th of a second or less. It follows, therefore, that electronic flash is most suitable for hand-held exposures while a tripod may be necessary when the illumination is supplied by photofloods or natural lighting.

Although electronic flash is virtually instantaneous, it does not penetrate as well as light from flash bulbs. The fall off in colour, therefore, behind the subject which is focused will inevitably be greater when electronic flash is used. That is a very important point to remember.

Each method of lighting has its keen supporters. Electronic flash is certainly the easiest to use and most economical if a large number of pictures are proposed but electronic flash, like flash bulbs, produces harsh shadows which cannot be avoided. For the most pleasing results, photoflood lighting is to be preferred, the drawback of this method being that it tends to destroy spontaneity because it is impossible to photograph a person without that person being aware that a photograph is being taken. On the other hand, electronic flash pictures or flash bulb pictures frequently make the subject look startled.

The whole subject resolves itself into a matter of personal choice. For the amateur who can hold a camera still for 1/30th of a second and who is not proposing to take a large number of indoor subjects, expendable flash bulbs are probably to be preferred, especially as the blue flash bulb can be used successfully with outdoor film and no filter.

CHAPTER 8

Looking at Your Colour Pictures

There is no difficulty in looking at paper prints made from colour negatives. You can treat them in the same way as black and white photographs, with the reservation that the colour values are adjusted to viewing in daylight. That only means that in artificial light the prints will look slightly unnatural because the nature of artificial light and daylight is different, so that the rendering of colours in the prints also appears different.

It is more complicated in the case of transparencies, that is, the products of reversal film. In this case there is not only the matter of viewing but also of preserving them. After processing, the majority of transparencies are returned mounted in card, or with card mounts supplied in which the transparencies can be placed. Card mounts are satisfactory for all practical purposes but if the transparencies are to be projected frequently they should be mounted in glass, which prolongs their life indefinitely and insulates them from the heat of the projector lamp. Their colours, however, are not resistant to daylight any more than they are to heat. Transparencies, and also colour paper prints, should be stored in a cool dry place and should be exposed to light and heat only when they are being viewed. That is a matter of common sense but is often neglected. Even monochrome prints fade when stored and the same result must be expected of colour prints and transparencies. In the case of transparencies, however, if they are mounted in glass fading occurs only after a period of years, and they are capable of being projected hundreds of times without appreciable loss of colour.

Numerous hand-held viewers are on the market at prices ranging from a few shillings upwards. They are available both for 35 mm. and $2\frac{1}{4}'' \times 2\frac{1}{4}''$ transparencies. No one, however, could say with honesty that the hand-held viewer is the right answer to the question " what is the best way of seeing my colour transparencies? " Even if it were, viewers of this kind have the disadvantage that they can be used by only one person at a time, so that the satisfaction of sharing the pleasure one takes in the pictures with other people is diminished. This is especially true, of course, when a number of people want to see the pictures at the same time.

Only two pieces of equipment are necessary for viewing transparencies at their best—a projector and a screen, and of these by far the more important is the projector. More than two hundred projectors are on the market, ranging in price from less than £10 to more than £100. As in the case of cameras, because the market is so competitive, all are good value for money and it is impossible to recommend one in preference to another. The most important thing to bear in mind is the size of the room in which the transparencies are to be projected. Good results can be obtained with a projector taking a 100 or 150-watt lamp in a small room. If the slides are to be projected in a large room a 300-watt projector is essential and for a small hall or lecture room a 500-watt or even a 1,000-watt lamp is required.

One of the less expensive projectors is the Agfa CP 44, which with a 150-watt lamp costs approximately £15. For use with a 300-watt lamp, and with blower attachment to prevent damage to the slides, it costs slightly over £22. The Aldis 300, which accepts a 300-watt lamp, is also marketed at little more than £20, while the Aldis 303, a more advanced version of the 300, is marketed at less than £25. The Aldis 500, which is equipped for a 500-watt pre-focused lamp and suitable fan for cooling, is also on the market at less than £25 and can be used in the largest of rooms or in a small hall.

One of the more expensive of the Aldis range is the 5-Star 1000, which can be used with lamps up to 1,000 watts. It has a dual voltage motor and a very fine lens, and represents the best value that can be obtained for approximately £30. Equally the Aldis Super Six, with a 1,000-watt lamp and synchronymous motor blower for cooling is one of the best of the projectors which can be obtained for less than £50. It must be remembered, however, that the 1,000-watt lamp is not necessary unless the slides are to be projected in a very large room or a hall for public viewing.

A cheaper version of the Aldis Super Six with a similar $f/2·8$ lens to that incorporated in the Super Six 1000 is designed for use with a 300-watt lamp and is the better of the two models for projection in a room of moderate size. It costs about £30. Though the Super Six was designed primarily for photographers using 12 on 120 roll film, giving transparencies $2\frac{1}{4}''$ square, it can also be used to project 35 mm. transparencies.

The Aldis XT 150 is one of the cheaper projectors with semi-automatic operation and gives what is called magazine loading. This means that it is unnecessary to handle each slide individually, since the slides can be loaded into the magazine and the projector accepts them in the pre-determined order after the operation of the slide-changing lever. This is undoubtedly the simplest and quickest way to project slides with the certainty that they will remain in their pre-arranged sequence. There is also less danger of damage to the slides, since they are housed in individual frames for protection against dust and dirt. The XT 150 is supplied with a 150-watt lamp and is, therefore, only suitable for use in relatively small rooms, but its price is less than £20 and it is a surprisingly economic model for semi-automatic viewing. It is normally fitted with an 85 mm. $f/2\cdot5$ lens but 100 mm., 130 mm., and 150 mm. lenses are available at extra cost.

The XT 360 is a much more elaborate projector which gives fully automatic projection with remote control. Its manufacturers claim with good reason that it incorporates almost every feature which the enthusiastic user can demand. Its power-operated remote controls allow both slide changing and focusing to be carried out without handling the machine. The automatic self-timer projects a full magazine of slides at predetermined intervals but any slide may be kept on the screen for a longer period by means of the remote control. This projector is fitted with a 300-watt lamp, while a rheostat switch on the control panel allows the normal voltage of the lamp to be reduced, so permitting the user to vary the intensity of light to suit the transparency and incidentally extend the life of the lamp.

An unusual feature is a built-in socket for coupling the changer mechanism to a tape recorder so that the projection of the slides can be synchronised with a recorded commentary or music. An accessory kit to enable two magazines to be linked permits uninterrupted projection of 60 slides. This model, which costs rather more than £50, is suitable only for 35 mm. slides or super slides and not for $2\frac{1}{4}''$ square transparencies. A younger brother of the XT 360 is the XT 330, which costs approximately £40. It has many of the same features as its elder brother but has no self-timer, rheostat, or built-in relay contacts.

Many cheaper models are available. The Kodak range, for instance, represents extraordinarily good value. The Kodaslide Home Projector, which accepts a 150-watt lamp, costs about £10 and is well suited to projection in a relatively small room. 35 mm. slides are shown 30″ × 40″ at a distance of 10 feet. Bantam Colorsnap slides and super slides are slightly larger. The lens is an f/3·5 Ektanon, which gives a very clear picture, and slides are fed in at the top of the projector, so minimising the risk of jarring it. Focusing is unusually easy, while a knob locks the projector at any angle up to 10 degrees from the horizontal.

The Kodaslide 40 projector, which costs about £3 more than the Home projector, is a more advanced version of the same model. It has a similar f/3·5 Ektanon lens, a 150-watt projection lamp, and a similar condenser system. Like the Home projector, too, it accepts slides from the top, but as each new slide is inserted it pushes its predecessor down to be stacked automatically in a chamber at the base.

The Kodaslide 50 projector, though costing well under £20, is even more versatile. It is similar to the Kodaslide 40 but is a fan-cooled model with a 300-watt lamp. It can be made semi-automatic with the clip-on Kodamat rapid slide changer, while a remote control motor can be added to the slide changer, allowing what the manufacturers call " press-button armchair control." However, if these accessories are added the cost is very much greater, the Kodamat automatic motor and cable costing approximately £12. Incidentally the " collection box " stacks 36 cardboard slides or 14 glass-mounted slides in the right order for replacing in their boxes.

These are only a very few of the standard 35 mm. projectors available. Some quite reliable ones are even cheaper. The Clubman Cub, for instance, which is fitted with a 150-watt lamp and accepts 35 mm. transparencies, costs about £7, though the projector is supplied in parts which must be assembled by the user.

The tendency in recent years has been towards automatic or semi-automatic control. The new Norimat, of which the retail price is less than £20, is fully automatic on the magazine but picture focusing is manually operated by means of a knob control on top of the projector, thus eliminating the necessity of turning the lens while the projector is in operation. This model is fitted with a Katagon $f/2 \cdot 8$ 85 mm. lens.

Only a little more expensive is the Noris Airflow 300 blower-cooled projector, fitted with an $f/2 \cdot 8$ Katagon 85 mm. lens. A low working temperature is assured by the efficient heat filter and the specially designed Airflow cooling system. The low temperature is most important, both for avoiding damage to the transparencies and for prolonging the life of the bulb.

Only a short time ago no projector could be purchased at a relatively low price for slides larger than 35 mm. ones. The position is changing and an increasing number of projectors are being manufactured to accept 12 on 120 transparencies, i.e. transparencies $2\frac{1}{4}'' \times 2\frac{1}{4}''$, in their appropriate mounts. The Noris 66, priced in the £20 range, is one of these. It has an $f/3 \cdot 5$ Ennar 150 mm. lens, is well ventilated, and accepts a 150-watt lamp. It shows a four-feet-square picture at a distance of 12 feet. For £2 extra it is possible to buy slide conversion equipment so that standard 35 mm. slides can also be shown. The 35 mm. slide carrier is quickly exchanged for the larger one and is placed in position over guide rails. It is advisable to purchase also an 85 mm. $f/2 \cdot 8$ Katagon projection lens complete with focusing mount and adapter for less than £8. This makes the image size and projection distance identical, whether 35 mm. or $2\frac{1}{4}'' \times 2\frac{1}{4}''$ transparencies are being projected, and converts the Noris into a truly universal instrument.

A more elaborate version of the same model is retailed at slightly more than £30. This is the blower-cooled Airflow 66, with 300-watt lamp. It has all the advantages of the other models, including an $f/3·5$ Ennar 150 mm. lens, and represents excellent value for money. The main difference between this model and the Noris 66 is that the 300-watt lamp gives more brilliant images and is suitable for larger rooms.

The Gnome range of projectors is also well established. One of the most popular is the Litemaster 2×2, i.e. 35 mm. projector, which incorporates a very easy system of projection and can be made semi-automatic. Like several other projectors on the market, the automatic Litemaster can be built up in stages from the basic manually operated instrument. This means that the expense of an automatic projector can be spread over as long as the purchaser desires, while the perfectly efficient manual instrument is available at the time of the first purchase. Another advantage of the Litemaster is that it offers an unusual combination of lightness allied with strength and rigidity. 85 mm. or 100 mm. lenses can be fitted according to the size of the room. There is a heat absorbing filter to protect the optical unit, which can be removed quickly and easily for cleaning. The slide changer unit is also of an advanced design, while the manufacturers claim that the prototype instrument completed more than half a million changes without attention. Cooling of the slides is by means of a motor driven fan.

The Litemaster accepts either a 300-watt or 500-watt lamp, though if a 500-watt lamp is chosen the instrument requires the addition of a second heat filter. As on several other projectors described, there is an efficient tilt adjustment, while the engineers responsible for this model have gone a long way towards protecting the lamp from electrical surge, which shortens the life of projection lamps more than any other factor.

A motor unit is supplied for changing the slides, either as a separate unit or as an integral part of the model. Control

Pictures which are evocative of the spirit of the countryside often make good subjects for colour. Here the oast houses and the farm buildings take added interest from the figure in the foreground. *Agfacolour film. Photo by Christopher Trent.*

Something of the quality of an aerial view is suggested by pictures photographed from a neighbouring hill or, in the case of the seaside, a cliff. The land-locked harbours of Devon and Cornwall, of which Mevagissey is typical, offer splendid opportunities for this kind of treatment. *Ferraniacolor film. Photo by Christopher Trent.*

This photograph illustrates what can be achieved by the use of available light indoors with a really high-speed colour film. The exposure chosen was correct for rendering the girl in red. The greens in the garden are over-exposed, the colours in the interior of the room under-exposed, but the general effect is good and is one which could not be achieved without using a film of considerable latitude. *Kodak High-Speed Ektachrome film.*

is by remote push-button and remarkably silent. This represents a major step towards a completely automatic projector which can be operated from an armchair and will show a succession of slides without manual operation. In the case of cameras, automation has many critics, but there can be no criticism in the case of projectors. The Litemaster is not cheap. The basic model with manual changer costs about £25, the extra heat filter for the 500-watt lamp and the automatic changer motor are sold separately.

However, there are many cheaper models in the same range, including the inexpensive Alphax I, which accepts a 150-watt lamp and costs less than £10. The Alphax can be converted into a projector accepting 300 or 500-watt lamps by adding the Gnome fan base, and has an $f/3\cdot5$ 85 mm. lens suitable for projection in a small room and an adequate system of convection cooling. The Alphax II is a slightly more advanced instrument, costing about £2 more. It also accepts a 150-watt lamp, with a choice between an 85 mm. and a 100 mm. lens, both lenses being $f/2\cdot8$, in contrast with the $f/3\cdot5$ lens of the Alphax I. Although, like the Alphax I, it is designed as a 150-watt model, it is convertible for use with 300- or 500-watt lamps by the use of the Gnome fan base.

The Alphax III, which is still well under £20 in price, actually incorporates the Gnome fan base as an integral part and accepts a 300-watt lamp, which gives enough light for projection on a normal screen in quite a large room. In other respects it is similar to the Alphax II, with the same choice between the 85 mm. and 100 mm. $f/2\cdot8$ lenses. It can also be converted for use with 500-watt lamps by inserting an additional heat filter, while an automatic slide changer can be used with the help of a simple adapter. The total price of the basic projector with 500-watt lamp and extra heat filter, the adapter for

113

automatic changer, and the automatic changer, is little more than £25. The Alphax IV is a newer model, slightly more expensive, which incorporates all the advantages of the Alphax III with some additional refinements. It, too, is designed primarily to accept a 300-watt lamp but can be converted without difficulty to accept a 500-watt one.

All these Alphax 35 mm. models are now available with an automatic slide changer as an integral part. The magazine will accommodate 36 card-mounted transparencies, while each slide compartment is numbered serially for the purpose of identification. It is simple in use and when the Alphax projector is purchased with the automatic slide changer, the adapter is included in the price. The projector with automatic slide changer costs approximately £5 more than the manually operated model. Additional magazines can be obtained for less than 10/- and a whole evening of viewing can be achieved with remote control, the magazines being filled in advance and the only activity on the part of the projector being to change the magazines.

That brings us to the Alphax Major, a recent addition to this range and one which conforms to the marked tendency to manufacture projectors which will accept a 12 on 120, i.e. $2\frac{1}{4}'' \times 2\frac{1}{4}''$ transparency as well as the standard 35 mm. one. $2\frac{1}{4}'' \times 2\frac{1}{4}''$ transparencies are normally mounted in $2\frac{3}{4}'' \times 2\frac{3}{4}''$ slides and the Alphax Major is designed primarily to take this size. In other respects it is similar to the Alphax III and Alphax IV, accepting a 300 or 500-watt lamp, containing an efficient heat filter which must be duplicated if a 500-watt lamp is fitted, an adapter for 35 mm. slides, and an $f/3\cdot5$ 150 mm. lens. A high-speed electric motor produces powerful blower cooling. Part of the airstream produced by the motor is directed over the transparencies. Universal in the case of projectors means one thing and one thing only—the capacity to project $2\frac{1}{4}'' \times 2\frac{1}{4}''$ slides and 35 mm. ones. At little more than £25 the Alphax Major is one of the most economical of such universal projectors.

A recently introduced projector, the Rollei Universal Projector, also accepts $2\frac{1}{4}'' \times 2\frac{1}{4}''$ slides as well as 35 mm. ones and super slides. The price of this is approximately £80, which puts it outside the scope of ordinary holiday snapshotters. One feature of this projector is that by means of two magazines placed on either side one can project at will either 35 mm. transparencies or $2\frac{1}{4}''$ square transparencies. This is also an automatic projector which can be controlled by a cable at a distance of 10 feet, though longer cables are available if it is desired to operate the projector in a hall or lecture room. A Zoom lens is in course of production with a variable focal length from 110 to 160 mm. The purpose of this is to produce projected pictures of equal size whether the transparencies are $2\frac{1}{4}'' \times 2\frac{1}{4}''$ or 35 mm. The additional cost of this Zoom lens is more than £40.

The Rollei Table Projector is a most interesting innovation though of more limited appeal. It works in conjunction with any Rollei 6×6 camera with a detachable focusing hood and a standard lens of 75, 80 or 135 mm. focal length. The camera becomes part of the projector. The focusing hood is removed and the camera locked in position on the projector. Then the viewing lens of the camera serves as the projector lens and is focused by means of the camera focusing knob. Incidentally it is possible to use the camera for projection while it is loaded with film.

The projector accepts a standard 6 volt, 35-watt car lamp which, apart from being very economical, has an extremely long life. With the normal 12 on 120 size transparency a picture of $18'' \times 18''$ is obtained on the screen but special Rolleinar lenses can be obtained to provide larger projected pictures of up to 40″ × 40″. By means of an adapter supplied as an accessory, it is possible to project the standard 35 mm. transparency or the 4 cm. by 4 cm. super slides. A small-size projection screen 18″ × 18″ is available for table viewing.

The basic price of this projector with slide carrier, flex, and bulb is about £20, the accessory slide carrier for super slides little more than £1, while the Rolleinar lenses for larger projections are all under £3. The 35-watt lamp for the table projector costs less than 4/- and the 18″ × 18″ projection screen approximately £3. This represents exceptionally good value for viewers who do not wish to project their slides on to a large screen.

A similar but even cheaper table projector is the portable model known as the Companion. The advantage of this projector is that it is very light in weight and can be taken to show friends one's latest transparencies in their own homes. It takes less than a minute to erect and projects a picture on the built in screen slightly less than one foot square, the screen being situated within the case lid. If a screen is available and a larger picture desired, the lid can be removed quickly and a picture 40″ square or more projected. This remarkable little instrument, which accepts a 150-watt lamp, costs about £20, including the lamp and semi-automatic magazine slide changer. With a conventional slide changer it is about £5 cheaper.

The Prado is a very high-quality projector manufactured by Leitz (Instruments) Ltd. The most expensive types are ideal instruments for projecting small-size transparencies on to large screens in lecture halls but, like the Rollei Universal Projectors, they cost more than most amateurs either want or need to pay. The most advanced is the Prado 500, which takes a 500-watt lamp, has a built-in silent blower which cools the slides as well as the lamp, and can be supplied with lenses varying from 90 mm. in focal length to 250 mm. The standard lens supplied is one of 150 mm. focal length, the cost being about £60, excluding the lamp. An attachment is available for converting this for $2\frac{1}{4}'' \times 2\frac{1}{4}''$ transparencies with a different lens at a price of slightly under £40. Generally when lectures are being given in large halls the best lens is one with a focal length of 200 mm., which gives a well illuminated and unusually well-defined picture up to 17 feet square in size from a 35 mm. transparency.

There are cheaper models in the Prado range which yield a very high degree of definition and are equally reliable in use though not capable of projecting such a large image over so long a distance. The Prado 150 is designed for 35 mm. slides. It is fitted with a standard 100 mm. $f/2\cdot8$ lens of high quality, uses a 150-watt lamp, and is retailed at little more than £20. The Prado 250, which is similar to the 150 but accepts a 250-watt lamp, is retailed at between £35 and £40. This model also has the advantage of interchangeable lenses varying from 90 mm. in focal length to 150 mm. An attachment is available, too, as with the Prado 500, for conversion to the projection of $2\frac{1}{4}'' \times 2\frac{1}{4}''$ transparencies.

The Prado 66 is designed especially for $2\frac{1}{4}'' \times 2\frac{1}{4}''$ transparencies mounted in $2\frac{3}{4}'' \times 2\frac{3}{4}''$ slides, and accepts a 250-watt lamp. It is retailed at about £45, and is about £10 more expensive when fitted with a conversion attachment for a 500-watt lamp. This model can also be converted for the projection of 35 mm. slides with a separate lens for about £30.

Although the projectors described in the previous pages represent only a small selection of the models available, they can be regarded as representative. The more one pays, the better the picture, but it is wasteful to buy a projector for use in a small room at a cost appropriate to one whose performance is suitable for use in a lecture hall. As in the case of cameras, the chief difference between projectors is the quality of the lenses, but the lenses fitted to the cheaper projectors are adequate for the work for which they have been designed in almost every case. There may be some lack of definition in the case of the very cheapest models, perhaps some falling off of quality towards the edges of the pictures projected, but these are not faults which are obvious to people looking at the projections from a distance of a few feet. In a large room or a lecture hall a far higher quality of sharpness is necessary and, therefore, a higher quality lens is essential.

The other main difference between one model and another is the wattage of the lamp for which they are designed. Here the position is rather different. One can obtain a reasonable image with a 150-watt lamp in a small room but an infinitely better one with a 300-watt lamp, which renders the colours of the transparencies with greater brightness and brings out the detail much better. In a larger room a 500-watt lamp is a great advantage.

Automatic slide changers are a luxury but a very pleasant one. Doubtless in the course of a few years they will become cheaper and more projectors will be fitted with them as an integral part of the model. Apart from these three factors—the lens, the lamp, and special attachments such as the automatic slide changer—one projector is very like another. The determining factors are solely the amount that one is prepared to pay and the size of the room in which it is proposed to use the projector. In this connection the following table supplied by Gnome Photographic Products of Cardiff for Alphax projectors is of interest. It shows the picture size which is obtained with the use of 85 mm., 100 mm. and 150 mm. lenses at varying distances from the screen.

118

| LENS | DISTANCE | | |
	6 ft.	9 ft.	13 ft.
35 *mm.*			
85 mm.	21 × 32 in.	32 × 48 in.	47 × 80 in.
100 mm.	18 × 27 in.	27 × 40 in.	40 × 60 in.
2¼″ *square*			
150 mm.	29 × 29 in.	44 × 44 in.	60 × 60 in.

This table will help you to choose the focal length of your projector lens in relation to the size of the room in which projection will normally be made and the size of the screen available.

" What shall I put my projector on? " is the insistent query of many people who have no experience of projecting transparencies. The answer to this simple question is not so simple. It is possible to place the projector on a table or on a chair piled up with books and the results may be quite satisfactory, but this is another case of spoiling the ship for a ha'p'orth of tar. Surely if one is buying a relatively expensive projector it is worth providing also a stand which will allow it to function at its maximum efficiency. The stand need not be particularly expensive. The most simple stand for a projector is a tripod which should not cost more than £5. The only necessary requirements are that it should be completely rigid and capable of adjustment to various heights so as to make projection on a screen easy at any height which the user may desire. These tripods are portable and are usually capable of extension to a height of about 3 feet 6 inches or 4 feet.

Many more elaborate stands are available. In the Nebro

119

range, for instance, a strongly made and rigid stand with an adjustable tilt and with one leg extendable to deal with uneven floors is available for about £7, with an additional shelf for slides which are not being used at the time. The Nebro " Chair " projector stand can be clamped to most chair-backs or to any vertical surface and also has an adjustable tilt and is marketed at about £4. The Cambridge with a height of 45″, is marketed at approximately £13. The London projector stand is a more elaborate version. It has a rigid top surface in plastic and, like the others, a shelf for spare magazines. It is adequate for carrying any projector, while its normal height is 45″, but it costs well over £30, a price which is far too high for the average amateur, though it is admirable for use with small epidiascopes or film projectors.

The only important thing is that the projector should be based on a solid foundation and it should be capable of adjustment without varying its " tilt." For ordinary purposes the tripod type is adequate, even though the more solidly based type of stand may be theoretically more satisfactory and may give better results if projection is intended in a very large room or lecture hall. The difference in cost, however, is so great that the amateur who only desires to project his slides to a small audience may be well advised to choose the cheaper type.

When transparencies are projected a number of the points which have been explained in earlier chapters of this book will be apparent. It will be obvious, for instance, that it is essential to separate the important parts of a picture from the unimportant parts, or, in other words, to concentrate on the main focus of interest. If a transparency is viewed in daylight this is much less obvious but when a major enlargement is made on a screen the truth of the point is underlined.

It will be equally obvious that it is often useful to minimise the amount of sky, partly because the blue of a clear sky tends to dominate a picture, and partly because even a dramatic sky can detract from the subject of a photograph. It will be apparent, too, that the advice given for choosing a raised viewpoint is good, if only because a raised viewpoint often is the best means of isolating the main subject of interest from a background cluttered with inessential details. That is only another way of saying that the simplest motifs are often the most effective and that close-up shots of detail are frequently more rewarding in the finished picture than a whole scene.

If one can use a wide-angle lens, as with a Leica or similar camera, it will give a great depth of field as well as width to the picture, a very great advantage in the case of many subjects, including landscapes.

When transparencies are projected it is obvious that unusual angles of view and viewpoints often make a well-known subject look different. This is equally true whether the subject being photographed is London Bridge or the harbour of San Francisco. A carefully chosen viewpoint can make pictures of them look original, even though thousands of photographs have been taken of them and their general appearance is known to most people.

Colour transparencies can be projected on to any light-coloured surface. The wall of a room, especially if it is painted or distempered white or cream, can provide a good surface. Many people use a sheet. But these are makeshift appliances which cannot be expected to give such good results as a specially designed screen. The screen is the true partner of the projector in ensuring the best possible results from transparencies.

Two kinds are available—the plain white screen and the screen which is variously described as beaded or " ground glass." There is no agreement among experts which gives the best results. Many professionals prefer the plain screen, but there is no doubt that the beaded screen gives a rather more brilliant picture, though there may be some distortion.

Both types are manufactured for standing on a table or with a tripod attachment, or for hanging on a wall from a picture rail. As in the case of buying a projector, it is largely a matter of deciding on the most suitable type in relation to the room in which the transparencies will be most often projected. That is also the prime consideration in deciding on the size of the screen to be bought. Prices vary according to the size and type from less than £2 to more than £20, while the choice is almost as bewildering as in the case of cameras or projectors. As an example, the Da-Lite screens, which are intended to be fitted to a tripod, the base of which is wide and adjustable to suit uneven floors, vary in price from £5 to £17 or more. The cheapest is 30″ × 40″ and has a beaded surface. The 40″ square model, approximately £1 more expensive, also has a beaded surface. The 50″ square model with a beaded surface costs £8, a better quality in the same format about £10, while the Lenticular surface screen, 40″ square, known as the Silver-Lite, is retailed at about £14, and the 50″ square model of the same type at about £17.

Other manufacturers produce highly competitive models. The Aldis range, for instance, includes several tripod screens which can be erected in a few seconds. The screen surfaces are coated with glass beads and the fine grain ensures fair resolution and definition. The 40″ square model is recommended for small to average-size rooms, and is retailed at about £6, the 50″ square model at about £8. This can be used in small halls as well as in larger rooms.

The Duomatic screens are more robust versions of the Aldis and can be used either as wall screens or tripod screens. The glass-beaded screen material is tougher than that of the Aldis screens and provides as good a surface for projection as any, but the prices are almost twice as great. The main advantages are that the finer beading minimises grain in the projected images, so giving clearer and sharper pictures.

The Cinepro standard screen is supplied either as a matt white screen with a top coating of silver paint, or as a glass-beaded screen. It is available in sizes ranging from 30″ × 22″ to 46″ × 35″ with prices ranging from less than £3 to about £5. This is a screen intended for use on a table top. The Lumaplak is one of the more expensive of popular screens. It is strongly made and beautifully finished and has an original type of self-erecting mechanism. The largest type provides a maximum picture size of 57″ × 57″. With a matt white finish it is retailed at approximately £20, and a glass-beaded model is about £4 more expensive.

One of the cheaper series of screens which have proved remarkably reliable is that marketed by R. F. Hunter Ltd. It includes the Safari screen, which is easily erected, very light-weight, and incorporates a steel bar for holding the surface taut. It is marketed in six sizes from 31″ × 23″ to 50″ × 50″, while the prices range from £3 to £5 according to the size. A light-weight stand is also on sale for the conversion of these Safari screens from table-top models into tripod screens at less than £2.

The really important point to remember when erecting and dismantling all these screens is that the surface must not be allowed to come into contact with any hard object liable to cause scratching or other damage. This is particularly important in the case of the Safari, in which the steel rod used to keep the surface taut can do irreparable damage if it is wrongly handled. It is equally necessary to avoid any pressure on the surface with the fingers when erecting or lowering the screen and this is even more important with a beaded screen than with one which has a plain matt surface. Damage can also be done by damp and in some cases by cold. The rule, therefore, is to store the screen in a warm dry room when it is not in use. It is by taking such precautions that the full pleasure of projecting transparencies can be achieved.

Finally, four partners share in making a picture. First, and most important, is the photographer; second, and not much less important, the camera; third, the projector; and last, the screen. If any one of these four is inadequate the result cannot be pleasing. That is by far the most important guide to the full enjoyment of photography in colour.